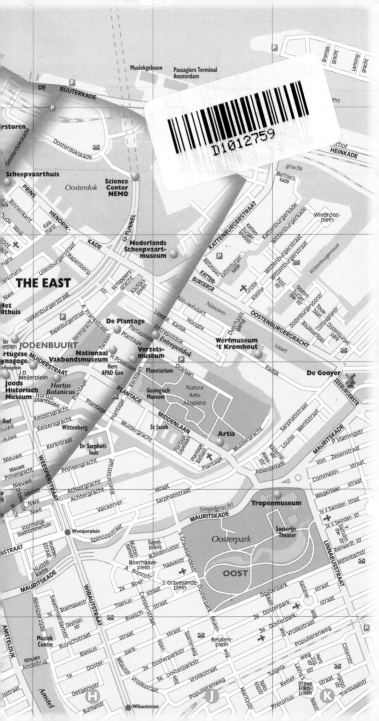

Musiekgebouw
Passagiers Terminal
Amsterdam

DE RUIJTERKADE

Brantas-
gracht

Lamong-
gracht

rstoren

Oosterdokskade

Oosterdokskade

HEINKADE

Scheepvaarthuis

gracht

Mariniers-
kade

PRINS

Oosterdok

Science
Center
NEMO

Windroos-
plein

Binnenkant

HENDRIK-

KADE

Oude Waal

Kalk-
markt

U-TUNNEL

Kattenburgerkade

Wittenburgerkade

KATTENBURGERSTRAAT

Kattenburgerkade

Wittenburgerkade

Wittenburgerstraat

Nederlands
Scheepvaart-
museum

Jeschans

Ullenburgerstr.

Rapenberg

Schippers-
gracht

Kadijks-
plein

KATTEN-
BURGERGR

Wittenburgervaart

THE EAST

Het
sthuis

Valkenburgerstraat

Rapenburgerstraat

A Frankstraat

Herengracht

Nieuwevaart

Grote

Kleine

OOSTENBURGERSTRAAT

Contr
leidr

Laagte Kadijk

Hoogte

Oostenburg

Oostenburgervoorstr.
Tour-
laan

Cortenelaar

park

Mr
erplein

JODENBUURT

De Plantage

Plantage
Plantagekade

Entrepotdok

Werfmuseum
't Kromhout

OOSTENBURGERGRACHT

rtugese
ynagoge

Nationaal
Vakbondsmuseum

Verzets-
museum

Entrepotdok

vaart

MUIDERSTRAAT

H Polaklaan

Kadijk

De Gooyer

J D
Meijerplein

Hers
APAD Gen

Plantage
Kerklaan

Planetarium

Doklaan

ZEEBURGERSTR

Joods
Historisch
Museum

Hortus
Botanicus

Hortus
plantsoen

PLANTAGE

Geologisch
Museum

Natura
Artis
Magistra

lhof
euwe

Keizersgracht

Plantage

MIDDENLAAN

Sarphatistraat

Wentstraat

MAURITSKADE

Nieuwe

Keizersgracht

Wittenberg

Muidergracht

St Jacob

Artis

Louise

Alex
str

P Vlamingstr

Von Zesenstraat

Kerkstraat

Dr Sarphati-
huis

Muidergracht

Plantage
Badlaan

Alex-
str

Commelin-
straat

Nieuwe
Prinsengracht

Prinsengracht

Plantage
Badlaan

Alexanderkade

Wagenaar-
straat

Nieuwe

Achtergracht

Reetenstr

Plantage

1e V Swinden- straat

Lepidu

Achtergracht

Valkenier-

straat

Sarphatistraat

Singelgracht

2e V Swinden- str

Nwe

Tropenmuseum

Reinwardt- str

Voormalige
Stadstimmertuin

Weesperplein

Spinozastraat

MAURITSKADE

Oosterpark

Soeterijn
Theater

Wittenbachstr

STRAAT

Huddenstraat

Weesperzijde

Hudde-
kade

MAURITSKADE

WIBAUTSTRAAT

Salet-
plein

Boerhaave-
plein

Boonsstr

's-Gravesandestr

's-Gravesande
plein

's-Gravesandestraat

LINNAEUSSTRAAT

OOST

Oosterpark

2e Oosterpark-
straat

straat

AMSTELDIJK

Muziek
Centre

Swammerdamstr

1e Boerhaavestr

Deyman-
str

Ruyschstraat

Blasius-

1e Oosterpark-
straat

2e Oosterpark-
straat

Oosterpark

straat

Beukenweg

Vrolikstraat

Populierenweg

Cilliersstr

Nieuwe
Amstelbrug

straat

Oetgenstr

park-
straat

Tilanus-

2e Boer-

Campestr

Ruysch-

straat

2e Oosterparkstr

3e Oosterparkstr

Beuken-
plein

Vrolikstraat

Sumatrastr

3e Oosterparkstr

Populierenweg

Tugelaweg

Steve
Biko-
plein

Retiefstr

Pretorius-

Transvaalstr

Amstel

straat

Burmanstr

Vrolikstraat

Maurits-

Spaar-
kade

Laing's

Nagel

Wibautstraat

H   J   K

How to Use This Book

KEY TO SYMBOLS

➕ Map reference to the accompanying fold–out map

✉ Address

☎ Telephone number

🕐 Opening/closing times

🍴 Restaurant or café

🚉 Nearest rail station

Ⓜ Nearest subway (Metro) station

🚌 Nearest bus/tram route

⛴ Nearest riverboat or ferry stop

♿ Facilities for visitors with disabilities

❓ Other practical information

▷ Further information

ℹ Tourist information

✋ Admission charges: Expensive (over €10), Moderate (€5–€10), and Inexpensive (under €5)

★ Major Sight   ★ Minor Sight

👣 Walks   🚌 Excursions

🏬 Shops

🎵 Entertainment and Nightlife

🍴 Restaurants

This guide is divided into four sections

• Essential Amsterdam: An introduction to the city and tips on making the most of your stay.

• Amsterdam by Area: We've broken the city into five areas, and recommended the best sights, shops, entertainment venues, nightlife and restaurants in each one. Suggested walks help you to explore on foot.

• Where to Stay: The best hotels, whether you're looking for luxury, budget or something in between.

• Need to Know: The info you need to make your trip run smoothly, including getting about by public transport, weather tips, emergency phone numbers and useful websites.

Navigation In the Amsterdam by Area chapter, we've given each area its own colour, which is also used on the locator maps throughout the book and the map on the inside front cover.

Maps The fold–out map accompanying this book is a comprehensive street plan of Amsterdam. The grid on this fold-out map is the same as the grid on the locator maps within the book. We've given grid references within the book for each sight and listing.

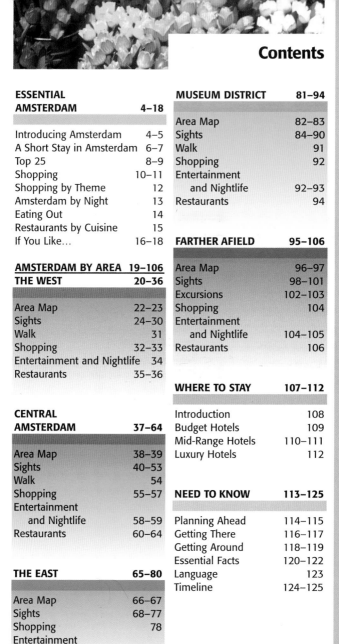

Contents

Introducing Amsterdam

How do you define Amsterdam? To some it's canals, carillons ringing out from church steeples and the variety of the Dutch gable. To others it's synonymous with tolerance—of eccentricity and of experimentation, of red light districts and smoking cafés.

Amsterdam is small—you can cross the city centre on foot in 30 minutes—and there are 750,000 people packed into not quite enough space. Yet it rewards frequent visits, and it has a changing schedule of special exhibitions, festivals and arts events—from the wackiest avant-garde shows to the works of Rembrandt and Vermeer. The many faces of Amsterdam help to make it among Europe's most popular short-break destinations.

The city feels like a big village. Amsterdammers' sociability makes it easy to get to know people—as does the fact that many speak several languages. Intellectual, curious about the world and great talkers, it is not surprising that Amsterdammers have dared to embark on some of the great social experiments of our time. It sometimes seems that where Amsterdam, with the rest of the Netherlands, leads, the world generally follows—though maybe a few centuries later. Prostitution has been tolerated in the city since the 17th century. Amsterdam's liberal drug laws allow licensed cafés to permit the sale of cannabis. The city invented traffic calming—tough laws and schemes to discourage cars and improve driving conditions—and it may yet become the first city to ban cars outright. Laws permit euthanasia and gay marriage. Informality is the norm—many local people long ago abandoned business attire, and most restaurants are unpretentious. A lot of street corners have a *bruine kroeg* (brown café), named after the mellow hue of the tobacco-stained walls where people settle down with a newspaper or argue over the issues of the day with friends and regulars.

Facts + Figures

- Bicycles—600,000
- Houseboats—2,500
- Windmills—6
- Canals—165
- Bridges—1,281
- Statues and sculptures—300
- Flower bulbs in parks—600,000

LIFE ON THE WATER

Amsterdam is expanding, to handle an expected population of 800,000 by 2020. Most expansion is among what used to be the quays and installations of the old harbour, many of them on artificial islands, along Het IJ waterfront. Cutting-edge architecture is the theme, but space has been kept for refurbished and repurposed warehouses and other buildings.

QUEEN'S DAY

Nothing better sums up Amsterdam than *Koninginnedag* (Queen's Day), the unstuffy monarch's official birthday (30 April) and the occasion for a wild citywide street party. Even radical Amsterdammers celebrate. Everyone wears orange, the royal shade, and the gay community dons tiaras, tinsel and fancy dress. More than a million people take part.

CYCLE CITY

Visitors may well be mown down by a speeding bicycle within a few moments of arrival. Designated cycle paths often run contrary to the traffic flow, so look both ways before crossing a road. Join in the fun on a bicycle without brakes– you have to back pedal. Never leave your bicycle unlocked. Free white bikes can be unlocked using an electronic smart card.

A Short Stay in Amsterdam

DAY 1

Morning Try to get to the **Anne Frankhuis** (▷ 24–25) when it opens at 9am, to avoid crowds The experience can leave quite an impression on visitors; afterwards a quiet canal stroll may be the order of the day. Make your way south down to the area of the **Jordaan** (▷ 29) known as the Negen Straatjes (Nine Streets), which straddle the canals from Singel to Prinsengracht. This district is full of interesting idiosyncratic shops.

Mid-morning Take a break on Huidenstraat at **Pompadour** (▷ 36), a chocolatier and tiny teashop. After wandering around here for while, make your way up to the pedestrianized Dam, the ceremonial and political heart of the city, dominated by the **Royal Palace** (▷ 45). The square is generally crowded and full of street entertainers.

Lunch On the northern side of Dam is the city's biggest department store, **De Bijenkorf** (▷ 55). You can get a tasty meal at the store's buffet-style restaurant, **La Ruche** (▷ 63), which offers a wide variety at a good price.

Afternoon After lunch, board a canal boat from the jetty on Damrak, near Centraal Station. For about an hour you can cruise around the canal ring, take photographs and listen to a commentary in several languages.

Early evening Most people are curious to see the **Red Light District** (▷ 49) and a visit just before dinner is probably the best time to do this. If you have any reservations about going, keep to the main drag, avoiding the dark side alleys, and you should feel quite at ease.

Dinner For a chic French meal try **Bridges** (▷ 60) in the Grand Hotel on Oudezijds Voorburgwal; for a less expensive Japanese option go to **Morita-Ya** (▷ 63) on Zeedijk.

DAY 2

Morning Start early at the **Rijksmuseum** (▷ 85), and although much is closed for renovation it is still possible to view Rembrandt's famous *Night Watch*. For modern art go on to the nearby **Van Gogh Museum** (▷ 88–89) to view the works of the master, but expect crowds, especially gathered around the *Sunflowers*. For those with an interest in drink rather than art make a detour to visit the **Heineken Experience** (▷ 90) on Stadhouderskade.

Mid-morning Take a break for coffee in the Van Gogh Museum before completing your tour of the masterpieces. Then go down to **Vondelpark** (▷ 87) for a breath of fresh air and a stroll in the park.

Lunch Take lunch at **Vertigo** (▷ 94) in the park. If the weather is fine, an outdoor table is a great place for people-watching.

Afternoon The park is the preferred green space of Amsterdammers and a popular place for joggers and walkers. With its 48ha (118 acres), it offers a welcome break from the hectic city life. Leave the park by the north end to walk to the smartest shopping street in the city, P. C. Hooftstraat. Here you will find international designer names as well as local Dutch designers. After some window-shopping or serious spending return to your hotel to freshen up.

Dinner Have an early-evening meal at **Brasserie Keyzer** (▷ 94) where musicians and concertgoers have been dining since 1903.

Evening Go next door to the magnificent **Concertgebouw** (▷ 93) for an evening of classical music or throw caution to the wind with a flutter at **Holland Casino Amsterdam** (▷ 93).

Top 25

►►►

Amsterdams Historisch Museum ▷ 40–41 The place to familiarize yourself with city history.

Anne Frankhuis ▷ 24–25 The young Jewish diarist's wartime refuge is sad yet inspiring.

Begijnhof ▷ 42 A haven of spiritual tranquillity and unhurried peace in the heart of the city.

Woonbootmuseum ▷ 28 Although a museum, this canal barge still feels like someone's home.

Westerkerk ▷ 27 Climb to the top of the tower for some great views across the city.

Vondelpark ▷ 87 This park throbs with life on a warm summer's day—great for people-watching.

Van Gogh Museum ▷ 88–89 You'll have to join the line to see the *Sunflowers* at this huge collection of van Gogh's work.

Tropenmuseum ▷ 98 The vivid, vibrant story of daily life in the tropics is told in this extraordinary museum.

Stedelijk Museum ▷ 86 This must for aficionados of modern art, is now back in its extended and revamped permanent home.

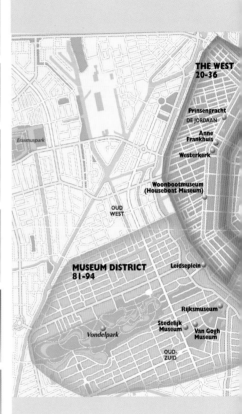

THE WEST
20–36

Prinsengracht
DE JORDAAN
Anne Frankhuis
Westerkerk

Woonbootmuseum
(Houseboat Museum)

Erasmuspark

OUD
WEST

MUSEUM DISTRICT
81–94

Leidseplein

Rijksmuseum

Stedelijk Museum

Van Gogh Museum

Vondelpark

OUD-
ZUID

Singel ▷ 50 Take a boat trip along the canal for the best view of the city and learn about its history.

Rosse Buurt ▷ 49 Most people just can't resist a look at the brazen Red Light District.

Rijksmuseum ▷ 85 The showcase of the artist Rembrandt and wonderful 17th-century Dutch art.

These pages are a quick guide to the Top 25, which are described in more detail later. Here they are listed alphabetically and the tinted background shows the area they are in.

CENTRAL AMSTERDAM 37–64

Het IJ

Herengracht
Singel
Nieuwe Kerk
CENTRUM
Koninklijk Paleis
Amsterdams Historisch Museum
Begijnhof
Bloemenmarkt
Museum Willet Holthuysen

Ons' Lieve Heer op Solder
Oude Kerk
CHINATOWN
Rosse Buurt

IJhaven
Oosterdok

THE EAST 65–80

Museum Het Rembrandthuis
JODENBUURT
Joods Historisch Museum

Amstel

Magere Brug

Nederlands Scheepvaart-museum

Natura Artis Magistra

Tropenmuseum

Oosterpark

OOST

DE PIJP

Sarphatipark

9

Shopping

Amsterdam is full of fascinating, quirky shops specializing in everything from toothbrushes to aboriginal art, children's comics to art deco lamps, potted plants to exotic cut flowers, jazz CDs to cheese, beer or African masks.

Off the Beaten Track

These character-rich shops are not always in the obvious places. Amsterdam's main shopping streets—Nieuwendijk and Kalverstraat—are dominated by global brands. Instead look where rents are lower: along Haarlemmerstraat, Damstraat and in the cross streets of the Canal Circle and the Jordaan. These cross streets were deliberately zoned for commercial use in the 17th century, when the canal circle was planned, and thrived on the trade in furs and hides. Just go and wander down Reestraat, Hartenstraat, Berenstraat, Runstraat and Huidenstraat among the medley of small specialist shops, cafés and art galleries, which have replaced the original furriers.

Individualists

The entrepreneurs who run these shops have a passion for their product and they want to share their enthusiasm, so customers are not treated merely as consumers, but as fellow connoisseurs. Some will spend all day talking about their sources. Others are busy making the products they sell—gorgeously decorated hats, Venetian-style masks, recycled vintage clothing, evening dresses or costume jewellery.

Clogs and tulips from Amsterdam are good gifts to bring home but don't forget the diamonds

---

CLOMPING CLOGS

Think Amsterdam and you'll probably think of clogs—or *klompen* as they are known in Dutch, a splendidly onomatopoeic word that imitates the heavy clomping sound the wooden shoes make as they hit the city's pavements. They are carved from a single block of poplar wood and are extremely comfortable. Most, however, are sold as decorative souvenirs rather than as footwear. You'll find them painted with windmills, tulips or cheeses.

Shopping with a Difference

The range of specialties and what they say about human ingenuity is incredible. For lovers of chocolate, try Pompadour (▷ 36). Feeling guilty consuming all that sugar? De Witte Tandenwinkel ('The White Teeth Shop'; ▷ 33) sells every imaginable style of toothbrush and every possible type of toothpaste. Olivaria (Hazenstraat 2A, tel 638 3552) is devoted to olive oils. Joe's Vliegerwinkel (Nieuwe Hoogstraat 19, tel 625 0139) sells only toys that fly—bright kites, boomerangs and Frisbees. Lovers of children's and adults' comics, new and second-hand, should visit Lambiek (▷ 33). Clogs are synonymous with the Netherlands, for a selection check out De Klompenboer (▷ 78). The city's fascination with the erotic has its stylish side in clothing from Absolute Danny (▷ 55).

Blooming Wonderful

You will find more flowers and bulbs in Amsterdam than in any other European city—not just in the floating flower market, but all around the Canal Circle. What better souvenir of your stay than a bouquet of blooms—always buy blooms that are still closed—or a packet of bulbs, but be sure to check the import regulations first.

FLEA MARKETS

The dark days of World War II engendered a habit of thrift in the citizens of Amsterdam, and even in today's prosperous times, no true Amsterdammer ever throws anything away. Instead, everything—from old light bulbs to ancient newspapers—gets recycled at one of the city's flea markets. The biggest and best known is the one on two sides of the Stadhuis (Town Hall) on Waterlooplein. Stalls here mix the new, the old and the unimaginably decrepit. Pick up very serviceable second-hand clothes, craft items and jewellery, and wonder why anyone would want to buy a broken radio, chipped vase or a doll without a head. Other flea markets include De Looier and the market at Noordermarkt.

Museum shops are a good source of souvenirs from the city. Cheese and plants are popular, too

Shopping by Theme

Whether you're looking for a department store, a quirky boutique, or something in between, you'll find it all in Amsterdam. On this page shops are listed by theme. For a more detailed write-up, see the individual listings in Amsterdam by Area.

ART AND ANTIQUES

Amsterdam Smallest Gallery (▷ 32)
Eduard Kramer (▷ 78)
Gastronomie Nostalgie (▷ 55)
Jaski Art Gallery (▷ 78)
De Looier Kunst- & Antiekcentrum (▷ 33)
Modern Art Market (▷ 78)
Premsela & Hamburger (▷ 57)

BOOKS

American Book Center (▷ 55)
Athenaeum Boekhandel (▷ 55)
Boekhandel Vrolijk (▷ 55)
Egidius Antiquarische Boekhandel (▷ 55)
De Kinderboekwinkel (▷ 33)
Selexyz Scheltema (▷ 57)
De Slegte (▷ 57)
Waterstone's (▷ 57)

DUTCH SOUVENIRS

Blue Gold Fish (▷ 32)
Bonebakker (▷ 55)
Dam Square Souvenirs (▷ 55)
Galleria d'Arte Rinascimento (▷ 32)
Gassan Diamonds (▷ 78)
Jorrit Heinen (▷ 33, 56)

FASHION

Absolute Danny (▷ 55)
Analik (▷ 55)
Blue Blood (▷ 92)
Broer & Zus (▷ 32)
Cora Kemperman (▷ 32)
Esprit (▷ 55)
Hester van Eeghen (▷ 56)
Oger (▷ 92)
Palette (▷ 57)
Retro (▷ 92)
Sissy-Boy (▷ 33)
Taft-Oscar (▷ 57)
Weber's Holland (▷ 57)

FOOD AND DRINK

De Bierkoning (▷ 55)
Geels en Co (▷ 56)
H. P. de Vreng (▷ 56)
Jordino (▷ 33)
Patisserie Holtkamp (▷ 78)
Pompadour (▷ 36)
Puccini Bomboni (▷ 78)
Van Avezaath Beune (▷ 92)
Vitals Vitamin-Advice Shop (▷ 57)
De Waterwinkel (▷ 104)

SPECIALIST SHOPS

Beadies (▷ 32)
De Beestenwinkel (▷ 78)
BLGK Edelsmeden (▷ 32)
Concerto (▷ 78)
Condomerie (▷ 55)
Cortina Papier (▷ 32)
Douglas Parfumerie (▷ 92)
Dreamlounge (▷ 32)

De Fietsenmaker (▷ 32)
Fifties-Sixties (▷ 32)
Frozen Fountain (▷ 32)
Den Haan & Wagenmakers (▷ 56)
Head Shop (▷ 56)
Hemp Works (▷ 56)
Hera Kaarsen (▷ 92)
Ivy (▷ 92)
Jacob Hooy (▷ 56)
Kitsch Kitchen Supermercado (▷ 33)
De Klompenboer (▷ 78)
Lambiek (▷ 33)
Mechanisch Speelgoed (▷ 33)
Nic Nic (▷ 56)
Otten & Zoon (▷ 104)
P.G.C. Hajenius (▷ 57)
Pol's Potten (▷ 104)
La Savonnerie (▷ 33)
Schaal Treinen Huis (▷ 104)
Shirdak (▷ 33)
De Witte Tandenwinkel (▷ 33)
Wonderwood (▷ 57)

STORES, MALLS AND MARKETS

De Bazaar (▷ 104)
Beethovenstraat (▷ 104)
De Bijenkorf (▷ 55)
Bloemen-en Plantenmarkt (▷ 78)
Magna Plaza (▷ 55)
Maison de Bonneterie (▷ 56)
Metz&Co (▷ 56)
Schiphol Plaza (▷ 104)
Vroom & Dreesmann (▷ 57)
Waterloopleinmarkt (▷ 78)

Amsterdam by Night

Amsterdam is one of Europe's most vibrant nightlife capitals. On a mild summer's evening nothing beats just walking by the canal, or gliding along the canals in a glass-topped boat, to see the historic bridges and buildings spotlighted in white lights.

Your Kind of Music

There is always something going on in the classical music world, most of it at the Concertgebouw (▷ 93) and the Beurs van Berlage (▷ 58). In addition, many churches host choral concerts and organ recitals, the Melkweg and Paradiso nightclubs (▷ 93) have rock and pop, Maloe Melo (▷ 105) has blues and rock, the Muziekgebouw aan 't IJ (▷ 105) has experimental music and, in an adjacent hall, Bimhuis (▷ 105) has jazz.

Out on the Town

The city's nightclubs offer all kinds of entertainment, including plenty that is explicitly erotic in the Red Light District with its sex shows and somewhat sleazy bars. Rembrandtplein throngs with preparty drinkers; they head for Escape (▷ 79), Rain (▷ 79) or the more sophisticated De Kroon (▷ 79) and Café Schiller (▷ 79). Leidseplein is another popular spot, with its lively street cafés and bars.

Something to Watch

There is plenty going on at the cinemas, both mainstream and art house. Don't miss the Pathé Tuschinski (▷ 59) in a splendid art deco building.

Take a stroll in the city at night–the illuminations brighten up the canals, bridges and buildings

---

CITY OF JAZZ

This is a city that adores jazz and blues, and there are scores of venues to chose from, including the legendary Bimhuis at the Muziekgebouw aan 't IJ and Maloe Melo. However, Amsterdam cedes to Rotterdam the privilege of hosting the renowned North Sea Jazz Festival that takes place in mid-July (www.northseajazz.nl) and attracts big international stars.

Eating Out

Choice is the key when eating out in Amsterdam. Gone are the days of establishments just serving rather stolid Dutch food. Take a look around and there is a great selection of 'fusion' cooking, a miscellany of tastes and a good range of prices.

Global Cuisine

Centuries of colonialism and a multicultural population are reflected in the city's cuisine. The most common of the ethnic cuisines are Indonesian and Chinese. Dutch colonists added their own dishes to the basic Indonesian meal, and most popular is the *rijsttafel*, which literally means 'rice table'. With rice as the focal point there can be anything from 15 to 30 dishes to accompany it. For more traditional Dutch food there are small intimate restaurants serving authentic cuisine (▷ below). There is however, a trend toward less heavy fare, a 'New Dutch' cooking, becoming increasingly popular.

Keeping the Price Down

If you are on a budget try the *eetcafés,* in which traditional Dutch food or more contemporary stylish dishes are served. Go for the *dagschotel* (dish of the day) or *dagmenu* (menu of the day). There's a good choice for vegetarians.

Practical Tips

Always reserve in advance for that special treat; restaurants tend to be small and fill up quickly. The Dutch like to eat early, 6.30–8, so restaurants get more full at this time. Eating out is a laid-back, casual affair; dress code only applies to the smartest of luxury and hotel restaurants.

AUTHENTIC DUTCH CUISINE

The most delicious dishes include *erwtensoep* (thick split-pea soup), *stamppot* (meaty stew), *gerookte paling* (smoked eel), *haring* (raw herring), *pannekoeken* (sweet and tasty pancakes), *stroopwafels* (waffles) and cheeses. The classic main course is *hutspot* (hotchpotch), another variation of stew.

There are plenty of unusual venues to take a meal in Amsterdam—on a canal or by a windmill

Restaurants by Cuisine

There are restaurants to suit all tastes and budgets in Amsterdam. On this page they are listed by cuisine. For a more detailed description of each restaurant, see Amsterdam by Area.

CAFÉS

1e Klas (▷ 60)
Café Americain (▷ 94)
Café Luxembourg (▷ 60)
Caffe Esprit (▷ 60)
Greenwood's (▷ 62)
Pompadour (▷ 36)
La Ruche (▷ 63)
Vertigo (▷ 94)

DUTCH

De Blauwe Hollander (▷ 35)
Brasserie De Poort (▷ 60)
Brasserie Keyzer (▷ 94)
Café de Fles (▷ 80)
Haesje Claes (▷ 62)
Keuken van 1870 (▷ 62)
Moeders Pot (▷ 35)
New Dorrius (▷ 63)
De Prins (▷ 36)
Spijshuis de Dis (▷ 106)
Steakhouse Piet de Leeuw (▷ 80)

ELEGANT DINING

De Belhamel (▷ 35)
Bridges (▷ 60)
Christophe (▷ 35)
Le Ciel Bleu (▷ 106)
Excelsior (▷ 62)
Le Garage (▷ 94)
De Gouden Reael (▷ 106)
Restaurant Bloesem (▷ 36)
La Rive (▷ 106)
De Roode Leeuw (▷ 63)
De Silveren Spiegel (▷ 64)

D'Vijff Vlieghen (▷ 64)
Vinkeles (▷ 36)

FISH

Albatros (▷ 35)
Brasserie Keyzer (▷ 94)
De Oesterbar (▷ 94)
Le Pecheur (▷ 63)
Visaandeschelde (▷ 106)

INDONESIAN

Aneka Rasa (▷ 60)
Bojo (▷ 35)
Indrapura (▷ 80)
Kantjil & de Tijger (▷ 62)
De Orient (▷ 94)
Sahid Jaya (▷ 64)
Sama Sebo (▷ 94)
Sarang Mas (▷ 64)
Tempo Doeloe (▷ 80)

INTERNATIONAL

Amsterdam (▷ 106)
Al Argentino (▷ 60)
De Brakke Grond (▷ 60)
Breitner (▷ 80)
Café Duende (▷ 35)
Café Pacifico (▷ 60)
Chez Georges (▷ 62)
Cinema Paradiso (▷ 35)
Dynasty (▷ 62)
Fromagerie Crignon Culinair (▷ 62)
In de Waag (▷ 62)
De Kas (▷ 106)
Memories of India (▷ 63)
Ocho Latin Grill (▷ 63)

Pakistan (▷ 106)
Pier 10 (▷ 63)
Pinto (▷ 80)
Riaz (▷ 94)
Rose's Cantina (▷ 63)
Segugio (▷ 80)
Semhar (▷ 36)
Sherpa (▷ 36)
Shibli (▷ 64)
Tango (▷ 64)
Teppanyaki Nippon (▷ 64)
Tokyo Café (▷ 64)
Toscanini (▷ 36)
Tuynhuys (▷ 64)
Le Zinc... et les Autres (▷ 80)

SNACKS AND *EETCAFÉS*

Bagels & Beans (▷ 94)
Baton Brasserie (▷ 35)
Gare de l'Est (▷ 106)
Het Karbeel (▷ 62)
Morita-Ya (▷ 63)
Pancake Bakery (▷ 35)
Small Talk (▷ 94)
Van Puffelen (▷ 36)

VEGETARIAN

Golden Temple (▷ 80)
Hemelse Modder (▷ 80)
Latei (▷ 63)
De Vliegende Schotel (▷ 36)

If You Like ...

However you'd like to spend your time in Amsterdam, these top suggestions should help you tailor your ideal visit. Each suggestion has a fuller write up elsewhere in the book.

A DUTCH MOMENTO

Tulips from Amsterdam and many other flowers and plants from the Bloemenmarkt (▷ 43).
For clogs to wear or replica souvenirs it is worth the trip to Otten & Zoon (▷ 104).
Handpainted Delftware plates, vases and more from Jorrit Heinen (▷ 33).

SHOPS WITH CHARACTER

If you are into the retro look in your home go to Fifties–Sixties (▷ 32) or Nic Nic (▷ 56).
Everything made of hemp? It's true at Hemp Works (▷ 56).
Herbs, spices and homeopathic remedies in this 1743 old-fashioned apothecary, Jacob Hooy (▷ 56).

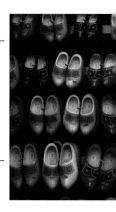

Brightly painted clogs make great souvenirs (above); eating outside is popular (below)

HONEST DUTCH FARE

From smoked eel to stews, the cooking at New Dorrius (▷ 63) is first class.
Robust home cooking can be found at De Blauwe Hollander (▷ 35). You are guaranteed huge portions.
D'Vijff Vlieghen (▷ 64) brings a more modern, lighter touch to the sometimes heavy traditional Dutch food.

BUFFETS–INDONESIAN STYLE

For your minibuffet with a Javanese twist go to Kantjil & de Tijger (▷ 62).
For an all-vegetarian *rijsttafel* try Aneka Rasa (▷ 60) in Warmoesstraat in the heart of the Red Light District.
Plate after plate arrives in the Balinese setting of Sama Sebo (▷ 94).

Green Amsterdam—take out a bicycle, walk along the canal bank or stroll in one of the parks

A CANALSIDE VIEW

Stay at the Estheréa Hotel (▷ 110) for perfectly placed quiet spot overlooking Singel (▷ 50).

More river view than canal, but the opulent Hotel de l'Europe (▷ 112) has a great position.

Located on peaceful Keizersgracht, try the charming Canal House Hotel (▷ 110).

THE LIVE MUSIC SCENE

Don't miss the world-famous Concertgebouw (▷ 93) for classical music par excellence.

For the very best in live jazz and blues stroll down to Jazz Café Alto (▷ 34).

From rock to reggae check out Paradiso (▷ 93), for Amsterdam's best live music.

AMSTERDAM ON A SHOESTRING

The Stayokay hostel (▷ 109) by the Vondel Park is good value.

La Ruche (▷ 63) in De Bijenkorf department store (▷ 55) offers good value and a good view, too.

The world-renowned Concertgebouw was built in 1888 and designed by A. L. van Gendt (above)

If you intend to use public transportation a lot in a day or few days, buy one-day or multi-day tickets (▷ 118–119).

GOING OUT AND ABOUT

You can't go to Amsterdam without going on a canal cruise, by day or night (▷ 118, 119).

Walk, jog, skate or run around the Vondelpark (▷ 87), the city's preferred green space.

Rent a bike (▷ 119) and join the locals for the best way to get around the city.

Wertheimpark is guarded by two sphinxes (left)

STYLISH LIVING

Amsterdam's history is all about water and ships (below)

If you like boutique hotels with oodles of style, you will love the Dylan (▷ 112).
Classical chic at the canalside Christophe restaurant (▷ 35), serving high class French cuisine.

Take a tour around Coster Diamonds (▷ 90) and then choose your jewel.

ENTERTAINING THE KIDS

Take the Museum Boat out to Science Center NEMO (▷ 77), the copper-clad hands-on science museum.
All aboard the *Amsterdam*, a replica 17th-century Dutch East Indiaman (▷ 72–73).
Be prepared to be scared at Amsterdam Dungeon (▷ 51), with live shows, actors and a ride back in time.

QUIRKY MUSEUMS

The Tulip Museum (▷ 30) is the only museum in the world to be dedicated to Holland's ubiquitous flower.
Discover all about life aboard in the quaint Woonbootmuseum (▷ 28).
The unusual Tropenmuseum (▷ 98) has evocative displays from around the world.

THE BEST CANALS

The elaborate interior of the extraordinary Tropenmusem (above)

Herengracht (▷ 44)–if you take a boat trip you will go along here, but it's also great to walk beside.
Singel (▷ 50)–wider than most but there is lots of interest along its banks.
Prinsengracht (▷ 26)–check out the vibrant houseboats and the merchants' houses.

Brouwersgracht (Brewers' Canal) is lined with converted warehouses, which date back to the 17th century (right)

The western area of Amsterdam is probably the most photogenic and is where the
real soul of the city resides. This is very
much a locals' area, with beautiful canals,
lovely old houses and individual shops.

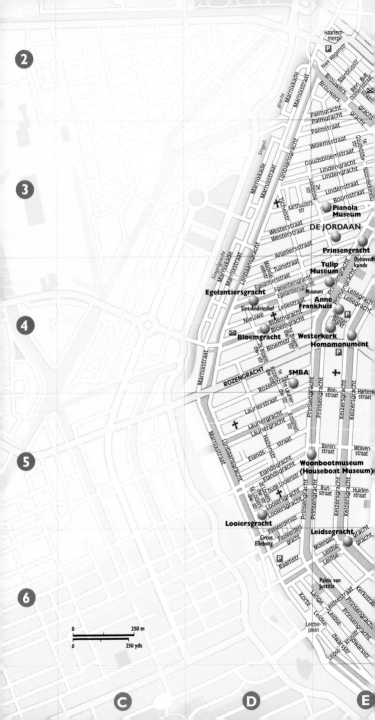

Haarlem-
merplf

Nwe Wagenstr

Bandnuijzer

Brouwers-
Brouwers-

gracht

Palmgracht
Palmgracht
Palmstraat

Willemsstraat

Goudsbloemstraat
Lindengracht
Lindengracht

Lindenstraat
Boomstraat

**Pianola
Museum**

Karthuizers-
str

Westerstraat
Westerstraat

DE JORDAAN

Anjeliersstraat

Prinsengracht

Tuinstraat

**Tulip
Museum**

Ophoved
kunde

Egelantiersgracht
Egelantiersgracht

Egelantiersgracht

Museum

Lellegracht

Sint-Andrieshof

**Anne
Frankhuis**

Nieuwe

Bloemgracht
Bloemgracht

Wester-
markt

Bloemgracht

Westerkerk
Homomonument

ROZENGRACHT

SMBA

Prinsengracht
Prinsengracht

Ree-
straat
Hartenstr

Laurierstraat
Lauriergracht
Lauriergracht

Elandsstr

straat

Elandsgracht
Elandsgracht

Oude Looiersstr

Beren-
straat
Wolven-
straat

**Woonbootmuseum
(Houseboat Museum)**

Rijn-
straat
Huiden-
straat

Looiersgracht
Looiersgracht

Looiersgracht

Keizersgracht
Keizersgracht

Passeerders
straat

Circus
Elleboog

Passeerders-
gracht

Leidsegracht

Molenpad

gracht

Leidse-

Raamstr

Leidse-

**Paleis van
Justitie**

Korte

Lange

Leidse-
plein

Leidsestraat
Leidse-

Prinsengracht

kerkstr

Leidse-
dwarsstr

Leidse kruiwarsstr

Marnixkade
Marnixstraat

Marnixkade
Marnixstraat

gracht

Singel-

Lijnbaansgracht

Marnixkade
Marnixstraat

Lijnbaansgracht

Marnixstraat

Lijnbaansgracht

0 ————— 250 m

0 ————— 250 yds

2

3

4

5

6

C

D

E

DID YOU KNOW?

● The Nazis occupied Amsterdam for five years.
● Of Holland's 140,000 pre-war Jewish population only 28,000 survived.

TIPS

● The experience of visiting does leave some visibly distressed—leave time to come to terms with what you have seen.
● The interactive video positioned at the end of the tour is often busy; if so, try the library instead.

'My greatest wish is to be a journalist, and later on, a famous writer...I'd like to publish a book called *The Secret Annexe*. It remains to be seen whether I'll succeed, but my diary can serve as a basis.'

Unfilled wish On Thursday 11 May 1944, just under three months before she was captured by the Nazis, Anne Frank wrote these poignant words in her diary. She never saw it published, but died in the concentration camp at Bergen-Belsen near the end of World War II, at age 15.

'The Secret Annexe' After Nazi Germany invaded the Netherlands in 1940, increasingly severe anti-Semitic measures were introduced. In 1942, the Frank and van Pels (van Daan) families, and Fritz Pfeffer (Alfred Dussel) went into hiding. For the

Clockwise from left: Waiting to see inside Anne Frankhuis is a time for reflection; the bookcase that hid the secret entrance where Anne and her family hid from the Nazis in 1942; it is difficult to believe that a family hid behind this plain facade for two years

next two years, Anne Frank kept a diary describing daily life and the families' fear of discovery—until they were betrayed to the Nazis in 1944. Her father was the only one of the group to survive. In 1947, following her wishes, he published her diary, calling it *Het Achterhuis* (*The Secret Annexe*).

Anne's legacy Around 500,000 visitors annually make their way through the revolving bookcase that conceals the entrance into the small, gloomy rooms so vividly described in the diary. Pencil lines mark the children's growth. The building is preserved by the Anne Frank Foundation, founded to combat racism and anti-Semitism and to promote 'the ideals set down in the Diary of Anne Frank'. In one entry Anne wrote: 'I want to go on living even after my death!' Thanks to her diary, this wish, at least, came true.

THE BASICS

www.annefrank.org

✚ E4

✉ Prinsengracht 267

☎ 556 7105

🕐 Mid-Mar to end Jun, first 2 weeks Sep Mon–Fri 9–9, Sat 9am–10pm; Jul–end Aug daily 9am–10pm; mid-Sep to mid-Mar daily 9–7

🚋 Tram 13, 14, 17. Stop/Go bus

🚤 Museum Boat North/South Line stop 2

♿ None

👊 Moderate

❓ 5-min introductory film

Prinsengracht

The handsome Prince's Canal (left) with its fine buildings including the Westertoren (right)

THE BASICS

➕ E3
🍴 Bars, cafés, restaurants
🚊 Tram 1, 2, 4, 5, 6, 13, 14, 16, 17, 24, 25. Stop/Go bus
🚢 Museum Boat North/South Line stop 2

HIGHLIGHTS

● Amstelkerk (▷ 75)
● Anne Frankhuis (▷ 24–25)
● Noorderkerk (▷ 30)
● Noordermarkt (▷ 30)
● Westerkerk (▷ 28)

DID YOU KNOW?

● Prinsengracht is 4.5km (3 miles) long, 2m (6ft) deep and 25m (80ft) wide to accommodate four lanes of shipping.
● A law (dating from 1565) restricts the lean of canal houses to 1:25.

Of the three canals that form the Grachtengordel (Canal Ring), Prinsengracht is in many ways the most atmospheric, with its fine merchants' homes, converted warehouses and flower-laden houseboats.

Prince William's canal Prinsengracht (Prince's Canal), named after William of Orange, was dug at the same time as Herengracht and Keizersgracht as part of a massive 17th-century expansion scheme. Together these three form the city's distinctive horseshoe-shape Grachtengordel (Canal Ring). Less exclusive than the other two waterways, with smaller houses, Prinsengracht became an important thoroughfare lined with warehouses and merchants' homes. Cargo would be unloaded from ships into fourth-floor storehouses by means of the massive hoist-beams seen today on the gables of many buildings (and still used for lifting furniture). Some houses were built with a deliberate tilt, to protect their facades from the goods as they were hoisted.

Floating homes Today, you'll also see some of Amsterdam's most beautiful houseboats, some with gardens, moored along Prinsengracht, near Brouwersgracht and alongside the ivy-covered quays close to the Amstel. Amsterdammers have long lived on houseboats, but the housing crisis after World War II skyrocketed the population of boat-people, so that there are more than 2,500 legal houseboats in Amsterdam, all with a postal address and power hook-ups. The unofficial figure is a lot higher.

The view from the church's clock tower, topped with a stunning crown, is panoramic

Westerkerk

This is the most beautiful of the four churches built in the 17th century to the north, south, east and west of the city's core. The views from the tall tower are superb and make the climb worthwile.

Masterwork The Amsterdam church most visited by tourists, has the largest nave of any Dutch Protestant church, and the tallest tower and largest congregation in the city. It is the masterwork of Dutch architect Hendrick de Keyser, who died in 1621, one year after construction began. Designed to serve the wealthy bourgeoisie living in the new mansions of the Grachtengordel (Canal Ring), it was eventually completed by his son Pieter with Cornelis Dancker in 1631. To its 85m (280ft) tower they added the gaudy golden crown—a symbol of the city granted by Habsburg Emperor Maximilian. The views over the Prinsengracht gables can be seen from the tower, popularly called 'Lange Jan' (Tall John). Outside the church, people often lay wreaths at the foot of the statue of Anne Frank, who used to listen to the church carillon while she was in hiding, before the bells were melted down by the Nazis.

Interior The simple, whitewashed interior is laid out in the shape of a double Greek cross. The massive organ is decorated with musical instruments and frescoes of the Evangelists by Gerard de Lairesse, one of Rembrandt's pupils. Rembrandt himself was buried here (in an unknown location) on 8 October 1669, as was his son, Titus, a year earlier in 1668.

THE BASICS

www.westerkerk.nl

🔲 E4

✉ Prinsengracht 281, Westermarkt

☎ Church 624 7766, tower 612 6856

🕐 Church Apr–end Sep Mon–Fri 11–3; tower Apr–end Sep Mon–Fri 10–5. Times vary and church may be closed at times stated

🚊 Tram 13, 14, 17. Stop/Go bus

🚤 Museum Boat North/ South Line stop 2

♿ Few

💶 Church free; tower moderate

❓ Carillon concerts most Tue at noon

HIGHLIGHTS

● Climb the tower
● Organ, Johannes Duyschot (1686)
● Anne Frank statue, Mari Andriessen
● Rembrandt memorial column
● Grave of Rembrandt's son

Woonbootmuseum

Once a working barge, this museum gives an insight into life on the water

See a houseboat inside

THE BASICS

www.houseboatmuseum.nl

⊞ D5

✉ Prinsengracht opposite No. 296, facing Elandsgracht

☎ 427 0750

🕐 Mar–end Oct Tue–Sun 11–5; Nov–end Dec, Feb Fri–Sun 11–5. Closed 1 Jan, 30 Apr, 25–26, 31 Dec

🍴 Café

🚊 Tram 13, 14, 17. Stop/Go bus

♿ None

💷 Inexpensive

HIGHLIGHTS

● Browse the houseboat library

● Watch the slide show

● Sip coffee in the café corner at the same eye level as the ducks

More than 2,500 houseboats line the canals of Amsterdam, homes to people who prefer an alternative lifestyle on the water. The Houseboat Museum explores the appeal of a floating home.

Home from home This museum—Houseboat Museum in English—feels exactly like someone's home, and the question that visitors most often ask is whether somebody still lives aboard the *Hendrika Maria*, a retired canal barge built in 1914. In fact, nobody does, but visitors are invited to pretend that they do: In this museum you are allowed to make yourself at home, sit in the comfortable armchairs and browse the books that line the walls of the surprisingly spacious living area.

High maintenance Another common reaction is: 'I'd love to live on a boat like this'. The museum provides plenty of information about houseboat living to encourage such dreams but warns about the rising price of moorings in Amsterdam. The slide show makes it clear that maintaining a houseboat is a work of love. Every three to four years the boat has to be taken out of the water and pressure hosed to remove corrosive accretions. Loose rivets have to be replaced and even whole sections of hull if they become thin.

Rising costs When all the costs are added up, houseboat living is not substantially cheaper than living in an equivalent-size apartment. But people who live on boats are passionate and would not have it any other way.

More to See

BLOEMGRACHT AND EGELANTIERSGRACHT
These are narrow canals in the Jordaan, a retreat from the downtown bustle, lined with pretty, small boats.
➕ D4 🚊 Tram 13, 14, 17. Stop/Go bus

BROUWERSGRACHT
Stretching from the Canal Ring into the Jordaan, Brouwersgracht owes its name to the many breweries established here in the 16th and 17th centuries. Houseboats and the old converted warehouses make this leafy canal particularly photogenic.
➕ E3 🚊 Tram 1, 2, 5, 13, 17. Stop/Go bus

HOMOMONUMENT
An arresting sculpture, the *Homomonument* (1987) is by Dutch artist Karin Daan. Consisting of three pink, granite triangles, the sign homosexuals were forced to wear during the Nazi occupation, it commemorates all those who have been persecuted because of their homosexuality.
➕ E4 ✉ Corner of Westermarkt and Keizersgracht 🚊 Tram 13, 14, 17

JORDAAN
This popular bohemian quarter with its labyrinth of picturesque canals, narrow streets, trendy shops, cafés and restaurants was once a boggy meadow alongside Prinsengracht.
➕ E3 🚊 Tram 3, 10, 13, 14, 17. Stop/Go bus

KEIZERSGRACHT
Together with Prinsengracht and Herengracht, this broad and elegant canal, built in 1612 and named Emperor's Canal after Emperor Maximilian I, completes the Grachtengordel (Canal Ring)—the trio of concentric central canals.
➕ E3 🚊 Tram 1, 2, 5, 13, 14, 16, 17, 24

LEIDSEGRACHT
One of the most exclusive addresses.
➕ E6 🚊 Tram 1, 2, 5, 7, 10. Stop/Go bus

LOOIERSGRACHT
In the 17th century, the main industry in the Jordaan was tanning, hence the name Tanner's Canal.
➕ D5 🚊 Tram 7, 10

Going to market in the attractive Jordaan district

Try your skills at Circus Elleboog

NOORDERKERK

This austere church, the first in Amsterdam to be constructed in the shape of a Greek cross, was built in 1620–23 for the Protestant workers in the Jordaan district. Noorderkerk is the venue for regular classical concerts.
➕ E3 ✉ Noordermarkt 44–48 ☎ 626 6436 🕐 Apr–end Oct Mon, Wed 10.30–3, Thu, Sat 11–1, Sun 1.30–5.30 🚋 Tram 1, 2, 5, 13, 14, 17. Stop/Go bus 🚻 Free

NOORDERMARKT

For a taste of the Jordaan district, head for the lively square surrounding the Noorderkerk. On Monday morning visit the Lapjesmarkt textile and second-hand clothing market, and on Saturday try the Boerenmarkt for organic produce, crafts and birds.
➕ E3 ✉ Noordermarkt 🕐 Mon–Fri 9–1, Sat 9–4 🚋 Tram 1, 2, 5, 13, 17

PIANOLA MUSEUM

www.pianola.nl
For something completely different visit the small Pianola Museum. There are nearly 20,000 music rolls in the museum archive; composers such as Mahler, Debussy, Ravel and Strauss recorded in this way. There are concerts in the museum every month.
➕ E3 ✉ Westerstraat 106 ☎ 627 9624 🕐 Sun 2–5. Group tours daily by appointment 🚋 Tram 13, 14, 17. Stop/Go bus 🚻 Moderate

SMBA

www.smba.nl
When the modern art in the Stedelijk Museum (▷ 86) is not latest-thing enough, try out the cutting-edge works at the Stedelijk's satellite gallery.
➕ D4 ✉ Rozenstraat 59 ☎ 422 0471 🕐 Tue–Sun 11–5 🚋 Tram 13, 14, 17 🚻 Free

TULIP MUSEUM

www.amsterdamtulipmuseum.com
This excellent little museum traces the history of the tulip from its origins in Central Asia. Round off your visit in the shop, selling every bulb imaginable.
➕ E4 ✉ Prinsengracht 112 ☎ 421 0095 🕐 Daily 10–6 🚋 Tram 13, 14, 17. Stop/Go bus 🚻 Inexpensive

Amsterdam is renowned for its beautiful tulips

A Walk into Jordaan

A pleasant stroll from the busy Dam to the pretty quiet canals of the west and on through the local district of the Jordaan.

DISTANCE: 4km (2.5 miles) **ALLOW:** 1–2 hours

START

DAM
🟦 F4 🚊 Tram 1, 2, 4, 5, 9, 14, 16, 24, 25

END

DAM
🟦 F4 🚊 Tram 1, 2, 4, 5, 9, 14, 16, 24, 25

THE WEST

WALK

1 Leave Dam via Paleisstraat; continue straight over the scenic Singel, Herengracht and Keizersgracht canals, and then turn right alongside Prinsengracht.

2 Pass Westerkerk (▷ 27) and Anne Frankhuis (▷ 24–25) and turn left on Leliegracht and cross Prinsengracht and double back for a few metres along the bank of the canal.

3 You will reach the peaceful Bloemgracht (▷ 29) canal. Turn right here, take the second right up Tweede Leliedwarsstraat, cross over Egelantiersgracht (▷ 29) and turn right along its shady bank.

4 Turn left up Tweede Egelantiersdwarsstraat into the heart of the bohemian Jordaan district, very much a local suburb with some unusual shops.

8 Continue across Nieuwezijds Voorburgwal, past the magnificent Nieuwe Kerk (▷ 46) on the left and return to the Dam.

7 Cross by the sluice gates and turn right along the eastern side of Singel, past Amsterdam's narrowest house facade (No. 7). To conclude the walk, turn left at Torensteeg, cross Spui and go along Molensteeg.

6 You come to attractive Brouwersgracht (▷ 29), lined with traditional barges and houseboats. Cross Brouwersgracht at Herengracht and walk along Brouwersgracht to Singel.

5 Walk on to Lijnbaansgracht, and then turn right on to Lindengracht, once a canal.

31

Shopping

AMSTERDAM SMALLEST GALLERY
www.smallestgallery.com
An original painting of the city bought here will remind you of your stay.
🞤 E4 ✉ Westermarkt 60
☎ 622 3756 🚋 Tram 13, 14, 17

BEADIES
www.beadies.com
Do-it-yourself jewellery: Choose from a huge range of vibrant beads to create your own designs.
🞤 E5 ✉ Huidenstraat 6
☎ 428 5161 🚋 Tram 1, 2, 5, 13, 17

BLGK EDELSMEDEN
www.blgk.nl
The showcase for a group of local jewellery designers, each one of whom takes a different contemporary approach to style, but all of them make distinctive pieces at moderate prices.
🞤 E4 ✉ Hartenstraat 28
☎ 624 8154 🚋 Tram 13, 14, 17

BLUE GOLD FISH
A Storehouse of fantastical gifts including jewellery, ornaments, home fixtures, fabrics and more.
🞤 D4 ✉ Rozengracht 17
☎ 623 3134 🚋 Tram 13, 14, 17

BROER & ZUS
www.broerenzus.nl
Delightful baby and toddler fashions for boys and girls up to the age of eight. They have their own designer label and carry other labels too. You can get some absolutely lovely baby shoes, and there are quality handmade toys, too.
🞤 D4 ✉ Rozengracht 104
☎ 422 9002 🚋 Tram 13, 14, 17

CORA KEMPERMAN
Stocks elegant and imaginative, fashionable yet bohemian, individually designed women's fashions.
🞤 E6 ✉ Leidsestraat 72
☎ 625 1284 🚋 Tram 1, 2, 5

CORTINA PAPIER
www.cortinapapier.nl
Visit to browse all kinds of notebooks, from plain to leather-bound, plus fine paper and writing materials.
🞤 E4 ✉ Reestraat 22
☎ 623 6676 🚋 Tram 6, 13, 14, 17

SHOPPING TIPS
Although Amsterdam does not compare with Paris or London for European chic, the large number of unusual specialist and second-hand shops and vibrant markets among its more than 10,000 shops and department stores, make shopping a real pleasure. Interesting souvenirs and gifts to take home are easy to find, whatever your budget. For shopping with a difference and a certain individuality, Amsterdam is hard to beat.

DREAMLOUNGE
This is just one of several shops that specialize in 'magic mushrooms'. It is part of the Conscious Dreams group, which also has a tattoo service.
🞤 E6 ✉ Kerkstraat 119
☎ 626 6907 🚋 Tram 1, 2, 5

DE FIETSENMAKER
One of the top bike shops in Amsterdam.
🞤 D5 ✉ Lauriergracht 50
☎ 625 8352 🚋 Tram, 13, 14, 17

FIFTIES-SIXTIES
www.fifties-sixties.nl
A jumble of period pieces including toasters, vacuum cleaners, records, lamps and other mementos of this hip era.
🞤 E4 ✉ Reestraat 5
☎ 623 2653 🚋 Tram 13, 14, 17

FROZEN FOUNTAIN
www.frozenfountain.nl
Not only is this striking interiors shop a dazzling showcase for up-and-coming Dutch designers, it is a fabulous place for finding unusual gifts, ceramics and jewellery.
🞤 E5 ✉ Prinsengracht 645
☎ 622 9375 🚋 Tram 1, 2, 5

GALLERIA D'ARTE RINASCIMENTO
www.delft-art-gallery.com
Visit this shop for all kinds, and quality, of Delftware, from the most expensive products of De Porcelyne Fles to cheap souvenirs, this piled-high shop also sells

excellent polychrome Makkumware.
🔲 E4 ✉ Prinsengracht 170 ☎ 622 7509 🚊 Tram 13, 14, 17

JORDINO
www.jordino.nl
Gorgeous creations in marzipan or chocolate, plus wonderful home-made ice cream.
🔲 E2 ✉ Haarlemmerdijk 25a ☎ 420 3225 🚊 Tram 1, 2, 5, 13, 17

JORRIT HEINEN
www.jorritheinen.com
Tiny but delightful for its Delftware plates, tulip vases and beautiful Christmas decorations.
🔲 E6 ✉ Prinsengracht 440 ☎ 627 8299 🚊 Tram 1, 2, 5, 13, 17

DE KINDER-BOEKWINKEL
www.kinderboekwinkel.nl
Children's books, arranged according to age.
🔲 D4 ✉ Rozengracht 34 ☎ 622 4761 🚊 Tram 13, 14, 17

KITSCH KITCHEN SUPERMERCADO
www.kitschkitchen.nl
Ghanaian metal furniture, Indian bead curtains, Mexican tablecloths, Chinese pots and pans—the whole world in one bright kitchen! An amazing variety of goods on sale including masses of plastic.
🔲 D4 ✉ Rozengracht 8–12 ☎ 428 4969 🚊 Tram 13, 14, 17

LAMBIEK
www.lambiek.net
This is the world's oldest comic shop, with a huge selection from around the world in many languages.
🔲 E6 ✉ Kerkstraat 132 ☎ 626 7543 🚊 Tram 1, 2, 5

DE LOOIER KUNST- & ANTIEKCENTRUM
www.looier.com
A covered antiques market with hundreds of stalls selling everything from quality items to junk. Open Saturday to Thursday 11–5.
🔲 D5 ✉ Elandsgracht 109 ☎ 624 9038 🚊 Tram 7, 10, 17

MECHANISCH SPEELGOED
Batteries are not included (they're not needed), in modern versions of classic toys from a kinder, gentler era of playthings.

🔲 E3 ✉ Westerstraat 67 ☎ 638 1680 🚊 Tram 3, 10

LA SAVONNERIE
www.savonnerie.nl
A veritable potpourri of bathtime products and accessories. You can even have your own personal text inscribed on the delicious handmade soaps.
🔲 D5 ✉ Prinsengracht 294 ☎ 428 1139 🚊 Tram 13, 14, 17

SHIRDAK
www.shirdak.nl
For something a bit different and for lovers of eastern textiles, try this interesting shop stocking products from Central Asia. Slippers, rugs, gifts, all in gorgeous hues. Also European felt hats, each one a unique design and a work of art.
🔲 D4 ✉ Prinsengracht 192 ☎ 626 6800 🚊 Tram 13, 14, 17

SISSY-BOY
www.sissy-boy.nl
Popular Dutch clothing chain with stylish, affordable clothing for men and women.
🔲 E6 ✉ Leidsestraat 15 ☎ 623 8949 🚊 Tram 1, 2, 5

DE WITTE TANDENWINKEL
www.dewittetandenwinkel.nl
Come here and discover just about everything you could want for your teeth.
🔲 E5 ✉ Runstraat 5 ☎ 623 3443 🚊 Tram 1, 2, 5, 13, 14, 16, 17, 24

Entertainment and Nightlife

BOURBON STREET
www.bourbonstreet.nl
Blues and jazz played nightly plus friendly staff create a good atmosphere. Love of good music brings fans of all ages.
E6 ✉ Leidsekruisstraat 6–8 ☎ 623 3440
🚊 Tram 7, 10

CAFÉ ROOIE NELIS
www.caférooienelis.nl
A taste of the old Jordaan bar culture, before yuppies, gentrifiers and New Agers arrived.
D5 ✉ Laurierstraat 101 ☎ 624 4167 🚊 Tram 13, 14, 17

CRISTOFORI
www.cristofori.nl
A shop that sells top-flight pianos extends its reach through concerts of classical, jazz and contemporary piano music.
E5 ✉ Prinsengracht 581–583 ☎ 626 8485
🚊 Tram 1, 2, 5

FELIX MERITIS
www.felixmeritis.nl
An important avant-garde dance and drama revue, and home to the Felix Meritis experimental theatre company.
E5 ✉ Keizersgracht 324 ☎ 623 1311 reservations; 626 2321 general information
🚊 Tram 13, 14, 17

HET MOLENPAD
The canalside terrace of this old-fashioned brown café catches the early evening sun.
E6 ✉ Prinsengracht 653 ☎ 625 9680 🚊 Tram 1, 2, 5

JAZZ CAFÉ ALTO
www.jazz-café-alto.nl
One of Amsterdam's best jazz and blues venues. Live music nightly; drinks are pricey.
E6 ✉ Korte Leidsedwarsstraat 115 ☎ 626 3249 🚊 Tram 1, 2, 5, 7, 10

JIMMY WOO
www.jimmywoo.com
This moody, dark bar and dance club embraces a high-maintenance chic that sees many people knocked back at the door.
D6 ✉ Korte Leidsedwarsstraat 18 ☎ 626 3150 🚊 Tram 1, 2, 5, 7, 10

PAPENEILAND
Amsterdam's oldest bar retains its old-world

ANCIENT AND MODERN
Brown cafés, so-called because of their chocolate-painted walls and dark wooden fittings, are reminiscent of the interiors in Dutch old master paintings. Here you can meet the locals in a setting that's *gezellig* (cosy). In stark contrast, there are a growing number of brasserie-like grand cafés, and chic, modern bars with stylish, spacious interiors. Watch also for the tiny ancient *proeflokalen* tasting bars (originally distillers' private sampling rooms), serving a host of gins and liqueurs.

charm with panelled walls, Makkum tiles, candles, benches and a wood-burning stove.
E3 ✉ Prinsengracht 2 ☎ 624 1989 🚊 Tram 1, 2, 5, 13, 17

ROZENTHEATER
www.rozentheater.nl
The Dutch plays and cabaret at this converted cinema might leave you in the dark, but the burlesque, dance and music are worth checking out.
D4 ✉ Rozengracht 117 ☎ 620 7953 🚊 Tram 13, 14, 17

SAAREIN2
www.saarein.nl
Originally founded as a women-only place, this café is now open to all but retains an emphasis on appealing to women.
D5 ✉ Elandsstraat 119 ☎ 623 4901 🚊 7, 10, 17

'T SMALLE
www.t-smalle.nl
Originally a *proeflokaal* (tasting house), from 1780, this cosy café has a terrace by the canal.
E4 ✉ Egelantiersgracht 12 ☎ 623 9617 🚊 Tram 13, 14, 17

DE TWEE ZWAANTJES
www.detweezwaantjes.nl
Traditional Dutch entertainment off the tourist track in a tiny bar full of accordion-playing, folk-singing Jordaaners.
E4 ✉ Prinsengracht 114 ☎ 625 2729 🚊 Tram 13, 14, 17, 20

Restaurants

PRICES

Prices are approximate, based on a 3-course meal for one person.

€€€ over €50
€€ €25–€50
€ under €25

ALBATROS (€€)

www.restaurantalbatros.nl
Eschews the fancy attitude affected by many seafood eateries, preferring to rely on its homey style and great seafood.

🔟 D3 ✉ Westerstraat 264, Jordaan ☎ 627 9932
🕐 Daily lunch, dinner
🚊 Tram 3, 10

BATON BRASSERIE (€)

A good choice for a quick, light lunch, this busy place serves salads, sandwiches and more, inside on two floors, and on a canalside terrace.

🔟 E4 ✉ Herengracht 82, Grachtengordel ☎ 624 8195
🕐 Mon–Fri 8–6, Sat–Sun 9–6
🚊 Tram 1, 2, 5, 13, 17

DE BELHAMEL (€€€)

www.belhamel.nl
Art nouveau style and classical music set the tone for polished Continental cuisine in an intimate, often crowded setting with a superb canal view.

🔟 E3 ✉ Brouwersgracht 60, Grachtengordel ☎ 622 1095
🕐 Dinner only 🚊 Tram 1, 2, 5, 13, 17

DE BLAUWE HOLLANDER (€)

www.deblauwehollander.nl
Generous portions of wholesome fare in a lively bistro setting.

🔟 E6 ✉ Leidsekruisstraat 28, Leidseplein ☎ 627 0521
🕐 Daily lunch, dinner
🚊 Tram 1, 2, 5, 7, 10

BOJO (€€)

www.bojo.nl
Popular late-night eatery serving rice, noodle dishes and satays. They serve good-size portions and plenty of vegetarian choices are available.

🔟 E6 ✉ Lange Leidsedwarsstraat 49–51, Leidseplein ☎ 622 7434
🕐 Mon–Fri dinner, Sat–Sun lunch, dinner 🚊 Tram 1, 2, 5, 7, 10

CAFÉ DUENDE (€–€€)

www.café-duende.nl
Authentic Spanish tapas

DUTCH TREATS

Numerous restaurants in the city provide a taste of authentic Dutch cuisine. Look out for the special 'Neerlands Dis' sign (a red, white and blue soup tureen), which indicates restaurants commended for their top-quality traditional Dutch cuisine. A modern trend is 'New Dutch' cuisine where traditional dishes are prepared with a lighter touch using fresh seasonal products and an adventurous mix of herbs and spices.

bar open late—food is served until 11.30. Daily specials, and a chef's plate if you want a blowout. There's a flamenco show on Saturday nights.

🔟 E3 ✉ Lindengracht 62, Jordaan ☎ 420 6692
🕐 Sun–Thu 4pm–1am, Fri–Sat 4pm–3am 🚊 Tram 3, 10

CHRISTOPHE (€€€)

www.restaurantchristophe.nl
Chef Jean-Joel Bonsens adds delicate touches from around the Mediterranean to a solid French foundation in his elegant canalside restaurant.

🔟 E4 ✉ Leliegracht 46, Grachtengordel ☎ 625 0807
🕐 Tue–Sat 6–10.30 🚊 Tram 13, 14, 17, 20

CINEMA PARADISO (€€)

www.cinemaparadiso.info
Spacious restaurant that attracts a cool crowd and serves honest Italian fare.

🔟 D3 ✉ Westerstraat 184–186, Jordaan ☎ 623 7344 🕐 Wed–Sun dinner from 6pm 🚊 Tram 3, 10

MOEDERS POT (€)

No-frills food is served at communal tables—chunky soups, casseroles, mussels, chicken and ham.

🔟 E2 ✉ Vinkenstraat 119, Jordaan ☎ 623 7643
🕐 Mon–Sat 5–9.30
🚊 Tram 10

PANCAKE BAKERY (€)

www.pancake.nl
The best pancakes in town, and a good place

to take the children with a choice of some 50 types of pancake. In the basement of an old canal house, it's a nice setting but you do need to like pancakes as there's really not much else.

➕ E4 ✉ Prinsengracht 191, Grachtengordel ☎ 625 1333 🕐 Daily 12–9.30 🚊 Tram 13, 14, 17

POMPADOUR (€)

The finest chocolatier in town doubles as a sumptuous tearoom. The tiny Louis XVI–style *salon de thé* is the perfect setting to eat your incredibly rich chocolate cakes.

➕ E5 ✉ Huidenstraat 12, Grachtengordel ☎ 623 9554 🕐 Mon–Sat 9–6 🚊 Tram 1, 2, 5

DE PRINS (€€)

www.deprins.nl
Very much of a local *eet-café* (café with eats), with an above-average restaurant that fills up fast, a cosy pub atmosphere and a seasonal menu.

➕ E4 ✉ Prinsengracht 124, Grachtengordel ☎ 624 9382 🕐 Daily 10am–1am 🚊 Tram 13, 14, 17

RESTAURANT BLOESEM (€€)

www.restaurantbloesem.nl
In a relaxed, informal yet chic atmosphere, there are two dining areas interconnected by arches. Choose from meat or game—try quail filled with red onion and pancetta or basil—fish or vegetarian

dishes such as marinated aubergine (eggplant) with mozzarella.

➕ E2 ✉ Binnen Dommersstraat 13, Jordaan ☎ 770 0407 🕐 Dinner only from 5pm 🚊 Tram 3

SEMHAR (€–€€)

www.semhar.nl
A wonderful example of Amsterdam's cultural diversity, this Ethiopian/Eritrean place has lots of vegetarian options, though the chicken stew is fantastic. So is the coffee, of course.

➕ D4 ✉ Marnixstraat 259-261, Jordaan ☎ 638 1634 🕐 Daily 4–10 🚊 Tram 10

SHERPA (€)

www.sherpa-restaurant.nl
Nepalese/Tibetan venue with traditional Himalayan ornaments. Nepalese meals are spicy; Tibetan dishes are prepared with noodles and ravioli.

DUTCH SUSHI

Long before Japanese sushi became fashionable fast food in Europe, the Low Countries already had their own version—raw herring, accompanied by chopped onion and pickles. Be sure to try some at one of the herring stalls dotted around town. Kromhout (✉ Junction of Singel and Raadhuisstraat), and Volendammer Viswinkel (✉ le van der Helststraat 60) are considered by locals as two of the best.

➕ E6 ✉ Korte Leidsedwarsstraat 58, Leidseplein ☎ 623 9495 🕐 Dinner only (lunch in summer) 🚊 Tram 1, 2, 5, 7, 10

TOSCANINI (€€)

The best Italian food in town. Reserve well ahead.

➕ E3 ✉ Lindengracht 75, Jordaan ☎ 623 2813 🕐 Mon–Sat dinner only 🚊 Tram 3

VAN PUFFELEN (€€)

www.goodfoodgroup.nl
A classic brown café that is a good restaurant, too. Wholesome French-style cooking is served in the panelled dining room.

➕ E5 ✉ Prinsengracht 375–377, Grachtengordel ☎ 624 6270 🕐 Daily noon–1am 🚊 Tram 13, 14, 17, 20

VINKELES (€€€)

www.dylanamsterdam.com
The ultra-chic restaurant of the Dylan Hotel (▷ 112) serves contemporary French cuisine with an international and fusiony twist.

➕ E5 ✉ Keizersgracht 384, Grachtengordel ☎ 530 2010 🕐 Mon–Fri lunch, Mon–Sat dinner 🚊 Tram 1, 2, 5

DE VLIEGENDE SCHOTEL (€€)

www.vliegendeschotel.com
Filling soups, salads, noodles and *rijsttafels* are on the menu here. Expect generous portions.

➕ D4 ✉ Nieuwe Leliestraat 162–168, Jordaan ☎ 625 2041 🕐 Daily 4–10.45 🚊 Tram 10

This is the heart of Amsterdam, the tourist hub with its medieval buildings, canals, main shopping streets and the upfront brashness of the Red Light District.

Amsterdams Historisch Museum

HIGHLIGHTS

● *View of Amsterdam*, Cornelis Anthonisz (1538), the oldest city map
● *The First Steamship on the IJ*, Nicolaas Bauo (1816)
● *Girls from the Civic Orphanage*, Nicolaas van der Waay (1880)
● Bell room

TIPS

● Make sure you get a plan of the musem as it can be easy to get lost without one.
● Browse the souvenir shop.

Try to make this lively and informative museum your first port of call, as once you have a grasp of Amsterdam's rich history, walking around the city is all the more rewarding.

The building This excellent museum traces the growth of Amsterdam from 13th-century fishing village to bustling metropolis, through an impressive collection of paintings, maps, models and historical objects. They are displayed chronologically in one of the city's oldest buildings. Originally a monastery, it was occupied by the city orphanage (Burgerweeshuis) for nearly 400 years, until 1975, when it was converted into a museum. Most of the present structure dates from the 16th and 17th centuries. Throughout, you can still see evidence of its former use—notably the ceiling

Clockwise from left: Detail from a plaque in the Amsterdams Historisch Museum; the former Burgerweeshuis for orphans, now the entrance to the musem; 19th-century pharmacy sign); suits of armour; brass weights and scales on display at the museum; market scene by P. Pietersz, 1610

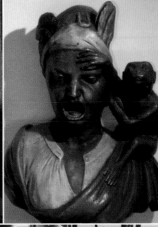

paintings in the Regent's Chamber and the numerous portraits of children, including Jan Carel van Speyck, who later became a Dutch naval hero.

The collections The first rooms of the museum chronicle the city's early history and its rise to prominence in trade and commerce. The displays include furniture, memorabilia and a map that illuminates each 25-year period of growth through the centuries. The main focus of the museum is the city's 17th-century Golden Age. Paintings and photographs illustrate the growing welfare problems of the 19th and early 20th centuries, and a small collection of relics from World War II shows how the Nazi occupation affected the population, 10 per cent of which was Jewish. A section focuses on the 'Modern City'. There are portraits of the Civic Guard in the adjoining Schuttersgalerij.

THE BASICS

www.ahm.nl
✚ F5
✉ Kalverstraat 92, Nieuwezijds Voorburgwal 357, Sint-Luciënsteeg 27
☎ 523 1822
🕐 Mon–Fri 10–5, Sat–Sun 11–5. Closed 1 Jan, 30 Apr, 25 Dec
🍴 David and Goliath Café
🚊 Tram 1, 2, 4, 5, 9, 14, 16, 24, 25
♿ Good
💰 Expensive
❓ Guided tours (1 hour) on request: call in advance

Begijnhof

TOP 25

The preserved buildings of the Begijnhof provided a sanctuary of peace

THE BASICS

www.begijnhofamsterdam.nl

✚ E5

✉ Gedempte Begijnensloot, entrance on Spui

🕐 Daily 9–5, enter chapel after 5pm via gate in Spui

🚊 Tram 1, 2, 5

♿ Good

💷 Free

❓ Shop

DID YOU KNOW?

● The last Begijn died in 1971.

● The Pilgrim Fathers are said to have worshipped here before leaving for England on the *Speedwell*, prior to crossing the Atlantic in the *Mayflower*.

● Today, the Begijnhof is a residence for single women earning less than €16,000 a year, and has a five-year waiting list.

Tranquillity characterizes the city's many *hofjes* (almshouses), none more so than this leafy oasis. The cobbled courtyard looks like a film set.

Pious women A tiny gateway leads to the Begijnhof, the oldest and finest *hofje* in the country (almshouses were charitable lodgings for the poor). This secluded community of magnificently restored old houses and gardens clustered around a small church lies a stone's throw from the main shopping thoroughfare. It was built in 1346 as a sanctuary for the Begijnen or Beguines, unmarried women who wanted to live in a religious community without becoming nuns. In return for modest lodging, they devoted themselves to the care of the poor and sick.

Two churches The Begijnenkerk (1419), dominating the courtyard, was confiscated from the Beguines during the Protestant Alteration in 1578. The women continued to worship secretly until religious tolerance was restored about 200 years later, in 1795. Meanwhile, their precious church became a warehouse until 1607, when it was given to the city's Scottish Presbyterian community and renamed (or misnamed) the Engelse Kerk (English Church). The simple interior has pulpit panels by Piet Mondrian. Nearby, Het Houten Huys (The Wooden House, 1425) is one of only two remaining wood-fronted houses in Amsterdam. It was built before 1521, when the use of wood as a building material was banned, after a series of fires.

Not just tulips in Amsterdam, the Bloememarkt has all kinds of plants on offer

Bloemenmarkt

Golden sunflowers, deep blue irises, delicately scented roses and row upon row of tulips and tulip bulbs—a vibrant blaze on the floating stalls of the flower market.

Floating market During the 17th and 18th centuries there were approximately 20 floating markets in Amsterdam, at least two of which gratified the Dutch passion for tulips. Nurserymen would sail up the Amstel from their smallholdings and moor here to sell their wares directly from their boats. Today, the stalls at this, the city's only remaining floating market, are permanently moored—and not all of the sales space is actually afloat. Offering a vast variety of seasonal flowers, plants, pots, shrubs and herbs, they are supplied by the florists of Aalsmeer and the region around Haarlem, at the horticultural heart of Holland. More than 16,000ha (39,540 acres) of the country are devoted to bulb growing.

Tulip mania Tulips were first spotted in Turkey by Dutch diplomats, who brought them back to Holland around 1600. Shortly after, a Leiden botanist discovered ways of changing their shape and hue, and tulip cultivation rapidly became a national obsession. Prices soared, with single bulbs fetching up to €1,360 (an average worker's annual salary was €68). Some were even exchanged for houses, and an abundance of still life paintings was produced to capture prize blooms on canvas. In 1637, the bubble burst, and many people lost entire fortunes. Prices are more realistic today and tulip bulbs are popular souvenirs for tourists.

THE BASICS

+ F6
- Singel, between Muntplein and Koningsplein
- Mon–Fri 9–6, Sat 9–5
- Muntplein
- Tram 1, 2, 4, 5, 9, 14, 16, 24, 25
- Good

HIGHLIGHTS

● The sights and smells are worth braving the crowds
● The best variety of tulips in the city as well as other types of plants and bulbs
● Decorative wooden tulips

Herengracht

Houses of all shapes and sizes, and with intricate gables, line the banks of Herengracht

THE BASICS

🔲 E4
🍴 Bars, cafés, restaurants
🚊 Tram 1, 2, 4, 5, 13, 14, 16, 17, 24, 25
🚤 Museum Boat North/South Line stop 2, 6

HIGHLIGHTS

● No. 43–45: Oldest warehouses (1600)
● No. 168–172: Theatermuseum and Bartolotti Huis
● No. 366: Bijbels Museum
● No. 409–411: 'Twin brothers' facing the 'twin sisters' (No. 390–392)
● No. 475: 'Jewel of Canal Houses'
● No. 497: Kattenkabinet (Cat Museum)
● No. 502: Huis met de Kilommen (Mayor's residence)
● No. 605: Museum Willet-Holthuysen (▷ 71)

DID YOU KNOW?

● If you stand on the bridge at the junction of Herengracht and Reguliersgracht, you can see 15 bridges simultaneously.

Exploring the city's grandest canal is like going back through time to Amsterdam's Golden Age. These gilded houses display four centuries of Dutch architectural styles.

The Gentlemen's Canal Herengracht takes its name from the rich merchants and traders of Amsterdam's heyday, and was the first of three concentric canals dug early in the 17th century to house the city's fast-growing population. Attracting the wealthiest merchant aristocrats, it has the largest, most ostentatious houses, 400 of which are now protected monuments. The houses had to conform to many building standards. Even the tone of the front doors—known as Amsterdam green—was regulated. As on all canals, taxes were levied according to the width of the canal frontage, hence the rows of tall, narrow residences.

Gable-spotting Canal-house owners expressed themselves in the elaborate decoration of their houses' gables and facades. The earliest and most common are the step gable and the spout gable. Amsterdam's first neck gable (No. 168) was built in 1638 by Philips Vingboons, and the bell gable became popular early in the 18th century. Around this time, Louis XIV-style facades were considered the height of fashion. No. 475 is a fine example—named the jewel of canal houses.

The Golden Bend Amsterdam's most extravagant mansions, with double fronts, were built between Leidsestraat and Vijzelstraat, along the stretch of the canal since dubbed the 'Golden Bend'.

The 17th-century Royal Palace, designed by Jacob van Campen, dominates the Dam

Koninklijk Paleis

Don't be put off by the Royal Palace's sober exterior. It belies the lavish decoration inside—a reminder of the wealth of Amsterdam in its heyday.

Civic pride At the height of the Golden Age, architect Jacob van Campen was commissioned to design Europe's largest and grandest town hall, and its classical design was a startling and progressive departure from the Dutch Renaissance style. The poet Constantijn Huygens called the Stadhuis 'the world's Eighth Wonder' and to this day it remains the city's only secular building on such a grand scale. Note the facade's astonishing wealth of decoration, numerous statues, an elaborate pediment and a huge cupola crowned by a galleon weather vane. During the seven years of construction, a heated argument developed as to whether a tower for the Nieuwe Kerk should have priority over a town hall. This was resolved when the old town hall burned down, and in 1655 the mayor moved into his new building.

Palatial wonder The town hall was transformed into a royal palace in 1808 after Napoleon made his brother Louis King of Holland. Today it serves as an occasional residence for Queen Beatrix, whose principal palace is in The Hague. The Tribunal, within the palace, was once the city's main courtroom, and condemned prisoners were taken from here to be hanged publicly on the Dam. This square has recently been pedestrianized and is a meeting place for locals and tourists, with the palace the major feature.

THE BASICS

www.paleisamsterdam.nl

☐ F4

✉ Nieuwezijds Voorburgwal 147, Dam

☎ 620 4060

🕐 Tue–Sun 12–5

🚊 Tram 1, 2, 4, 5, 9, 13, 14, 16, 17, 24, 25

♿ Good

💷 Moderate

HIGHLIGHTS

● Views of the Dam
● Tribunal
● Citizen's Hall
● Facade

DID YOU KNOW?

● The state bought the palace in 1936 for €4.5 million.
● It is 80m (265ft) long and 56m (125ft) wide.
● The bell tower is 51m (119ft) high.

Nieuwe Kerk

Overlooking the Dam is Niewe Kerk (left); fine monumental tombs (right)

THE BASICS

www.nieuwekerk.nl

➕ F4

✉ Dam

☎ 638 6909

🕐 Usually daily 10–6

🍴 Nieuwe Kafé

🚊 Tram 1, 2, 4, 5, 6, 9, 13, 14, 16, 17, 24, 25

⛴ Museum Boat North/ South Line stop 6

♿ Good

💶 Varies with exhibitions, but mainly expensive

❓ Regular organ concerts, mostly on Sun. Shop is open daily 10–6, until 10pm on Thu

HIGHLIGHTS

● Organ, Hans Schonat and Jacob Hagerbeer (1650–73)
● Organ case, Jacob van Campen (1645)
● Pulpit, Albert Vinckenbrinck (1644)
● Tomb of Admiral de Ruyter, Rombout Verhulst (1681)

Considering its turbulent history, it is something of a miracle that Holland's magnificent national church has survived. Hearing its organ is a real treat.

Not so new The 'New' Church actually dates from the 15th century, when Amsterdam was growing at such a rate that the 'Old' Church (Oude Kerk, ▷ 48) was no longer sufficient. Construction started in 1408 but the church was several times destroyed by fire. After the Alteration in 1578 (when Amsterdam officially became Protestant), and a further fire in 1645, the church was rebuilt and reconsecrated in 1648. It has no spire: Following years of debate, the money designated for its construction was spent to complete the close by Stadhuis (Town Hall), which is now the Koninklijk Paleis (▷ 45). It does have one of the finest of Amsterdam's 42 historic church organs—a Schonat-Hagerbeer organ, dating 1650–73, with 5,005 pipes and a full-voiced sound that easily fills the church's vast interior.

Famous names At the time of the Alteration, Amsterdam's churches were largely stripped of their treasures, and the Nieuwe Kerk was no exception. The altar space has since been occupied by the tomb of Holland's most valiant naval hero, Admiral Michiel de Ruyter, one of many names from Dutch history, including poets Peter Cornelisz Hooft and Joost van den Vondel. Dutch monarchs have been inaugurated here, from Willem I in 1815 to Beatrix in 1980. No longer a place of worship, it hosts exhibitions and recitals.

Golden candle lamp (left); the beautiful clandestine church of the museum (right)

Ons' Lieve Heer op Solder

Not only is this tiny museum one of the city's most surprising, it is also tucked away in a small, inconspicuous canal house close to the Red Light District.

Best-kept secret In 1578, when the Roman Catholic city council was replaced by a Protestant one, Roman Catholic churches were closed throughout the city. In 1661, while Catholic church services were still forbidden, a wealthy merchant named Jan Hartman built a residence on Oudezijds Voorburgwal, and two adjoining houses in Heintje Hoeckssteeg. He ran a sock shop on the ground floor, lived upstairs, rented out the spare rooms in the buildings behind, and cleverly converted the top two floors of the canal house and the attics of all three buildings into a secret Catholic church. Religious freedom only returned with the French occupation in 1795.

Hidden church This *schuilkerk* was just one of many clandestine churches that sprang up throughout the city, but it is one of only a few that has been completely preserved. It was saved from demolition in 1888 by a group of historians called the Amstelkring (Amstel Circle), who nicknamed the church 'Our Dear Lord in the Attic'. To find a three-level, galleried church at the top of a series of increasingly steep staircases is a surprising experience. Given that there is seating for 200 people, magnificent ecclesiastical statuary, silver chalices and other vessels, paintings, a collapsible altar and a huge organ, it is hard to believe that the services held here were really secret.

THE BASICS

www.opsolder.nl

➕ G4

✉ Oudezijds Voorburgwal 40

☎ 624 6604

🕐 Mon–Sat 10–5, Sun, public hols 1–5. Closed 1 Jan, 30 Apr

🚉 Centraal Station

🚊 Tram 1, 2, 4, 5, 9, 13, 16, 17, 24, 25, 26

⛴ Museum Boat North/ South Line stop 1, 7; Golden Age Line stop 1, 9

♿ None

💷 Moderate

❓ Occasional classical concerts in winter

HIGHLIGHTS

● Church of 'Our Dear Lord in the Attic'
● Altar painting *The Baptism of Christ*, Jacob de Wit (1716)
● Priest's bedroom
● Confessional
● Drawing room
● Kitchen

Oude Kerk

TOP 25

Dating back to the early 14th century, Oude Kerk is the city's oldest church

THE BASICS

www.oudekerk.nl

🔲 F4

✉ Oudekerksplein 23

☎ 625 8284

🕐 Mon–Sat 11–5, Sun 1–5. Closed 1 Jan, 30 Apr, 25 Dec

🚇 Nieuwmarkt

🚋 Tram 4, 9, 16, 24, 25

♿ Good

💲 Moderate

❓ Frequent organ recitals and carillon concerts

HIGHLIGHTS

● Great Organ, Vatermüller

● Stained-glass windows, Lambert van Noort (1555)

● Carillon, François Hemony (1658)

● The tombstone of Rembrandt's first wife, Saskia van Uylenburg, which is still in the church even though poverty drove him to sell her grave plot

Surrounded by cafés, bars and sex shops, the Old Church represents an island of spirituality in the Red Light District. Here brashness and purity rub shoulders.

History Amsterdam's oldest church, dedicated to St. Nicholas, the patron saint of seafarers, was built in 1306 to replace a wooden chapel dating from the late 1200s. Over the centuries, the church escaped the great fires that devastated so much of the city, and the imposing basilica you see today dates largely from the 14th century. Its graceful tower, added in 1565–67, contains one of the finest carillons in Holland. In the 16th century Jan Pieterszoon Sweelinck, Holland's best-known composer, was organist here.

Miracle In the 14th century, the Oude Kerk became one of Europe's pilgrimage hubs following a miracle: Communion bread regurgitated by a dying man and thrown on the fire would not burn, and the sick man did not die. Thousands of Catholics still take part in the annual *Stille Omgang* (▷ 114), a silent nocturnal procession, but as the Oude Kerk is now Protestant, it no longer follows the ancient pilgrim route to the church, going instead to the Begijnhof.

Sober interior The stark, impressive interior has a triple nave and elaborate vaulting. Three magnificent windows in the Lady Chapel survived the Alteration, as did the fine choir stalls. In the 1960s some delicate 14th-century paintings were found behind layers of blue paint in the vaults.

Rosse Buurt

You'll see plenty of neon in the Red Light District, Amsterdam's infamous tourist draw

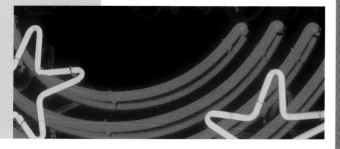

Amsterdam's Red Light District, bathed in a lurid red neon glow, and full of gaping tourists, junkies and pickpockets, is one of the city's greatest attractions.

Sex for sale As early as the 15th century, Amsterdam was infamous as a haunt of prostitution, and the lure of the Red Light District proves irresistible to many visitors to the city today. Crowds clog the narrow alleyways, sex shops, peep shows and suggestively named bars, while bored prostitutes beckon from their lighted windows. But there is more to the Red Light District than sex. 'Normal' people live here, too, and go about their everyday business in what, behind the tawdry facade, is an interesting part of the old city. The city council has cut the number of brothels and coffeeshops, replacing them with boutiques and other 'wholesome' businesses, in an effort to combat organized crime and people-trafficking.

Drug central The Red Light District is frequented by drug dealers, and hosts the majority of Amsterdam's marijuana-selling 'smoking' coffeeshops. The Hash Marihuana Hemp Museum on Oudezijds Achterburgwal traces the history of hashish and the cannabis plant.

Precautions Watch your wallet, avoid eye contact with undesirable characters, do not take photographs of prostitutes and avoid poorly lighted alleyways. Even though the evening is the liveliest time to visit, don't wander around alone. Be cautious in quiet areas at night, or avoid them completely.

THE BASICS

⊞ F4
✉ Borders roughly denoted by Zeedijk (north), Kloveniersburgwal (east), Damstraat (south) and Warmoesstraat (west)
🍴 Restaurants, bars, cafés
Ⓜ Centraal Station, Nieuwmarkt
🚃 Tram 4, 9, 14, 16, 24, 25

DID YOU KNOW?

● Possession of drugs is technically illegal but the authorities tolerate possession of up to 5g (1oz) of soft drugs (cannabis, hash and marijuana) for personal use.
● Drug-dealing is not allowed. 'Smoking' coffeeshops have to be licensed.
● There are some 600 'coffee houses' in Holland, of which around 200 are in Amsterdam, and some 30,000 'home-growers'.
● Brothels were legalized in 1990.
● Half of Amsterdam's prostitutes are foreign.

CENTRAL AMSTERDAM TOP 25

TOP 25

Singel

The tree-shaded Singel, once the city's first line of defence, is now a residential area

TOP 25

THE BASICS

- ✚ F4
- ✉ Singel
- ☎ Poezenboot 625 8794; www.pozenboot.nl
- ⏰ Poezenboot Thu–Tue 1–3pm
- 🍴 Cafés and restaurants
- 🚊 Tram 1, 2, 5, 13, 14, 17
- ♿ Poezenboot none
- 👜 Poezenboot free

HIGHLIGHTS

- Poezenboot
- Bloemenmarkt (▷ 43)
- Torensluis prison cell
- Munttoren (▷ 52)
- No. 7: narrowest house facade
- No. 2, 36, 74, 83: unusual facades

At first glance, this canal looks like any other major waterway in the city. Look a little closer, though, and you will discover some of Amsterdam's most unusual and enchanting sights.

Former city belt From its construction in the early 15th century until the late 16th century, the city limits were marked by the Singel (originally *Cingel*, meaning belt), the city's defensive moat. Then, in 1586, the city council decided to build quays along Singel's west bank and to convert the moat into a canal for freight ships. Thus Singel became the first of Amsterdam's concentric canals, and its curved shape established the horseshoe layout of the city. With the coming of the railways, canal transportation became less important and Singel began to acquire a residential character. Many warehouses are now converted into homes. The Nieuwe Haarlemmersluis, a sluice at the junction of Singel and Brouwersgracht, is opened nightly to top up the city's canals.

All that floats Perhaps the most unusual house is No. 7. The narrowest house front in Amsterdam, it was made no wider than a door in order to minimize property taxes. Opposite is the Poezenboot, a refuge for stray cats. Look out, too, for the Torensluis (Tower Lock, on Singel's widest bridge); in the 17th century it was used as a prison. The bridge has a monument to Multatuli (1820–87), one of the Netherlands' greatest writers. The floating flower market, the Bloemenmarkt (which doesn't entirely float), is on Singel.

More to See

AMSTERDAM DUNGEON
www.thedungeons.com
The latest of five dungeon attractions to open in Europe and scary too. It's the city's history with the 'horrible' bits. Live shows, actors, a drop ride into hell, a labyrinth and more.
➕ F5 ✉ Rokin 78 ☎ 530 8530 ⏰ Daily 11–5 🚊 Tram 4, 9, 14, 16, 24, 25 💷 Very expensive

BIJBELS MUSEUM
www.bijbelsmuseum.nl
Housed in two historic buildings known as the Cromhouthouses, this museum explores the world through one of the oldest and most read books in the world. You can relax in the lovely garden.
➕ E5 ✉ Herengracht 366–368 ☎ 624 2436 ⏰ Mon–Sat 10–5, Sun 11–5 🚊 Tram 1, 2, 5 💷 Moderate

BLAUWBURGWAL
Amsterdam's shortest canal extends between Singel and Herengracht, at Herenstraat.
➕ F4 🚊 Tram 1, 2, 5, 13, 17

CENTRAAL STATION
Many visitors get their first glimpse of Amsterdam's architectural wonders at Petrus Josephus Hubertus Cuypers' vast neo-Renaissance station (1889), standing with its back to the IJ inlet.
➕ G3 ✉ Stationsplein 🚇 Centraal Station

CHINATOWN
www.ibps.nl
Amsterdam's 7,000-strong Chinese community earns part of its living from the numerous Chinese restaurants around Nieuwmarkt. Take a look at the striking Fo Guang Shan He Hua Temple in Zeedijk, the largest Buddist temple in Europe.
➕ G4 ☎ Temple 420 2357 ⏰ Temple Tue–Sat 12–5 (also Mon Jun–Sep) 🚇 Nieuwmarkt

FRANCISCUS XAVERIUSKERK
This splendid neo-Gothic church is often dubbed *De Krijtberg* (Chalk Hill), because it is built on the site of a former chalk merchant's house.
➕ E5 ✉ Singel 442–448 ☎ 623 1923 ⏰ Services only 🚊 Tram 1, 2, 5

The main foyer of Centraal Station

HET IJ

Amsterdam is on precariously low-lying ground at the confluence of the IJ (an inlet of the IJsselmeer lake). During the city's 17th-century heyday, most maritime activity was centred on the IJ and along Prins Hendrikkade, where the old warehouses were crammed with exotic produce from the East. Since 1876 access to the sea has been via the North Sea Canal, and the industrial docks are now to the west. The IJ is busy with pleasure boats, barges, the free shuttle ferries to Amsterdam-Noord, from the Waterplein-West dock behind Centraal Station, and an occasional warship or visiting cruise liner.

🔲 F3 🚇 Centraal Station

HET LIEVERDJE

In the 1960s this little bronze statue of a boy ('Little Rascal'), in the middle of the square, became a symbol of the Provo movement, and main rallying point of anti-establishment demonstrations.

🔲 E5 ✉ Spui 🚊 Tram 1, 2, 5

MADAME TUSSAUDS

www.madametussauds.nl

See wax models of Rembrandt, van Gogh, Justin Timberlake and other characters from the 17th century to the present day, including US President Barack Obama, and an amazing 5m (16ft) giant clothed in windmills and tulips.

🔲 F4 ✉ Dam 20 ☎ 523 0623
🕐 Daily 10–5.30 (Jul–Aug to 8.30)
🚊 Tram 4, 9, 14, 16, 24, 25 ♿ Good
💰 Very expensive

MUNTTOREN

The tower of the former Mint was part of the southern gateway to the medieval city.

🔲 F6 ✉ Muntplein 🚊 Tram 4, 9, 14, 16, 24, 25

NATIONAAL MONUMENT

The 23m (75-ft) War Memorial obelisk on the Dam contains soil from the then 11 Dutch provinces and the colonies. Every year on 4 May the Queen lays a wreath here.

🔲 F4 ✉ Dam 🚊 Tram 4, 9, 14, 16, 24, 25

Dam Square's striking Nationaal Monument

Antiquarian books for sale at Oudemanhuispoort

OUDEMANHUISPOORT

Antiquarian bookstalls line this 18th-century arcade, between Oudezijds Achterburgwal and Kloveniersburgwal, part of the city's university.

➕ F5 ✉ Oudemanhuispoort ⏱ Mon–Fri 11–4 🚊 Tram 1, 2, 5

OUDEZIJDS ACHTERBURGWAL & OUDEZIJDS VOORBURGWAL

In contrast to most of the city's canals, parts of Oudezijds Achterburgwal and Oudezijds Voorburgwal are lined with glaring, neon-lighted bars and sex shops. Their southern sections are leafier, residential and adjoin the University of Amsterdam campus.

➕ F5 🚊 Tram 4, 9, 14, 16, 24, 25

POSTZEGELMARKT

Market for stamps, coins and medals.

➕ E5 ✉ Nieuwezijds Voorburgwal 280 ⏱ Wed, Sat 1–4 🚊 Tram 1, 2, 5

SCHREIERSTOREN

The Weeping Tower was where wives and girlfriends waved farewell to their seafaring menfolk. They had good reason to weep: Voyages took up to four years and many sailors died. Today the tower houses Café VOC, named for the Vereenigde Oostindische Compagnie (United East India Company) trading house.

➕ G4 ✉ Prins Hendrikkade 94–95 🚇 Centraal Station

SINT-NICOLAASKERK

www.nicolaas-parochie.nl

The main Roman Catholic church (1888) is one of many Dutch churches named after the patron saint of sailors.

➕ G4 ✉ Prins Hendrikkade 73 ☎ 684 4803 ⏱ Tue–Fri 11–4, Sat and Mon 12–3 🚊 Tram 1, 2, 4, 5, 9, 13, 16, 17, 24, 25, 26

ZEEDIJK

Once the sea wall of the early maritime settlement and until around 1990 a haunt of sailors and shady characters, this area on the fringe of the Red Light District is home to a parade of bars and restaurants.

➕ G4 🚇 Centraal Station 🚊 Tram 1, 2, 4, 5, 9, 13, 16, 17, 24, 25, 26

Detail of Schreierstoren, the Weeping Tower

Sint-Nicolaaskerk

Markets and Museums

A walk around the central area of the city, taking in some of the cultural venues, plus a chance to see some markets en route.

DISTANCE: 2km (1 mile) **ALLOW:** 1 hour

START

DAM
✚ F4 🚊 Tram 4, 9, 13, 14, 16, 17, 24, 25

1 Leaving the Dam via Paleisstraat, turn left on to Nieuwezijds Voorburgwal, where a stamp and coin market, Postzegelmarkt (▷ 53), is held.

2 About 100m (100 yards) farther on the left, Sint-Luciënsteeg leads to the excellent and informative Amsterdams Historisch Museum (▷ 40–41).

3 Pass through the Schuttersgalerij (Civic Guard Gallery) to Gedempte Begijnensloot. At the southern end, a stone archway on your right brings you into the Begijnhof (▷ 42) courtyard.

4 A further archway leads to Spui. On Friday, stalls sell old books, and on Sundays paintings. Head across the square and turn left along the edge of Singel (▷ 50).

END

DAM
✚ F4 🚊 Tram 4, 9, 13, 14, 16, 17, 24, 25

8 Ahead of you is the Nationaal Monument (▷ 52), a striking landmark on the Dam, bringing you back to the start of your walk.

7 The museum includes a fine Egyptian collection among its ancient cultural displays. Turn left after the museum over the canal and head first right up busy Rokin, with its antiques shops. At the end, on the left, is Madame Tussauds (▷ 52).

6 Your next landmark is the Munttoren (▷ 52) on the left at Muntplein. Cross over the canal (Rokin) and take first left on to Oude Turfmarkt where you will find the Allard Pierson Museum on your right with its collection of antiquities.

5 Cross the bridge on to Koningsplein to the popular flower market, the Bloemenmarkt (▷ 43).

Shopping

ABSOLUTE DANNY
www.absolutedanny.com
Erotic clothing and accessories with a distinctive design sensibility and a touch of class.
🔢 F5 ✉ Oudezijds Achterburgwal 78 ☎ 421 0915 🚇 Nieuwmarkt

AMERICAN BOOK CENTER
www.abc.nl
Four floors of English-language books, plus US and British magazines and newspapers. There is a good selection of books on Amsterdam.
🔢 F5 ✉ Spui 12 ☎ 625 5537 🚊 Tram 1, 2, 5

ANALIK
www.analik.com
Simple, elegant designs are the hallmark of this boutique belonging to Anakujm, considered Amsterdam's foremost young designer.
🔢 E4 ✉ Hartenstraat 36 ☎ 422 0561 🚊 Tram 1, 2, 5, 13, 14, 17

ATHENAEUM BOEKHANDEL
www.athenaeum.nl
This bookshop, in an art nouveau building, specializes in social sciences, literature and the classics, and stocks international newspapers.
🔢 E5 ✉ Spui 14–16 ☎ 514 1460 🚊 Tram 1, 2, 5

DE BIERKONING
www.debierkoning.nl
Beers and glasses from around the world.
🔢 E5 ✉ Paleisstraat 125 ☎ 625 2336 🚊 Tram 1, 2, 5, 13, 14, 17

DE BIJENKORF
www.debijenkorf.nl
The busy main department store, the 'beehive' lives up to its name.
🔢 F4 ✉ Dam 1 ☎ 0900 0919 🚊 Tram 4, 9, 14, 16, 24, 25

BOEKHANDEL VROLIJK
Stocking a broad range of gay and lesbian books in multiple languages, but mainly in English, Vrolijk is generally more affordable than the gay sections of mainstream bookstores.
🔢 F4 ✉ Paleisstraat 135 ☎ 623 5142 🚊 Tram 1, 2, 4, 5, 9, 13, 14, 16, 17, 24, 25

BONEBAKKER
www.bonebakker.nl
Holland's royal jewellers, with dazzling displays of gold and silverware. Enjoyable even if you can't afford to buy.
🔢 F5 ✉ Rokin 88–90 ☎ 623 2294 🚊 Tram 4, 9, 14, 16, 24, 25

CONDOMERIE
www.condomerie.com
The world's first specialist condom shop—fun but with a serious approach to hygiene and safe sex.
🔢 F4 ✉ Warmoesstraat 141 ☎ 627 4174 🚊 Tram 4, 9, 14, 16, 24, 25

DAM SQUARE SOUVENIRS
www.dutchsouvenirs.com
This souvenir shop has a choice of clogs, furnishings, wooden tulips, windmills, Delft pottery and T-shirts.
🔢 F4 ✉ Dam 17 ☎ 620 3432 🚊 Tram 4, 9, 14, 16, 24, 25

EGIDIUS ANTIQUARISCHE BOEKHANDEL
A tiny shop packed to the gunnels with antique books on travel, photography and the arts.
🔢 F3 ✉ Haarlemmerstraat 87 ☎ 624 3255 🚊 Tram 3

ESPRIT
www.esprit.com
Young, trendy designs for the seriously fashionable.
🔢 E5 ✉ Spui 10a ☎ 626 3624 🚊 Tram 1, 2, 5

GASTRONOMIE NOSTALGIE
www.gastronomienostalgie.nl
Specializes in antique

MAGNA PLAZA

Amsterdam's most luxurious shopping mall, Magna Plaza (www.magnaplaza.nl), is in an imposing neo-Gothic building, which was formerly the city's main post office, in Nieuwezijds Voorburgwal near the Dam. Its four floors are filled with upscale specialist shops, such as Pinokkio, for educational toys; Bjorn Borg, for sporty underwear; and the Henri Willig Cheese Gift Shop. There is a café on the top floor.

silver, silver-plated objects, porcelain, glass and crystal. This is the sort of tableware that was used in the heyday of hotels such as the Ritz, the Carlton and the Hotel de Paris.
⊞ E5 **✉** Nieuwezijds Voorburgwal 304 **☎** 422 6226 **🚊** Tram 1, 2, 5

GEELS EN CO
www.geels.nl
Holland's oldest coffee-roasting and tea-trading company is full of heady aromas, with helpful staff and a traditional setting.
⊞ F4 **✉** Warmoesstraat 67 **☎** 624 0683 **🚊** Tram 4, 9, 14, 16, 24, 25

DEN HAAN & WAGENMAKERS
www.dutchquilts.com
A quiltmaker's paradise of traditional fabrics, tools and gadgets. Closed Sunday to Wednesday.
⊞ F4 **✉** Nieuwezijds Voorburgwal 97–99 **☎** 620 2525 **🚊** Tram 1, 2, 5, 13, 17

HEAD SHOP
www.headshop.nl
The shop for marijuana paraphernalia and memorabilia ever since it opened in the 1960s.
⊞ G5 **✉** Kloveniersburgwal 39 **☎** 624 9061 **🚇** Nieuwmarkt

HEMP WORKS
www.hempworks.nl
Designer hemp shop: jeans, jackets, shirts, shampoo and soap all made of hemp.
⊞ F4 **✉** Nieuwendijk 13

☎ 421 1762 **🚊** Tram 1, 2, 5, 13, 17

HESTER VAN EEGHEN
www.hestervaneeghen.com
Handbags, wallets and other leather accessories in innovative shapes, styles and hues, designed in Holland and made in Italy.
⊞ E4 **✉** Hartenstraat 37 **☎** 626 9212 **🚊** Tram 13, 14, 17

H.P. DE VRENG
www.oudamsterdam.nl
Celebrated wine-and-spirits establishment, producing fine liqueurs and *jenevers* since 1852.
⊞ F4 **✉** Nieuwendijk 75 **☎** 624 4581 **🚊** Tram 1, 2, 5, 13, 17

JACOB HOOY
www.jacobhooy.nl
Old-fashioned apothecary,

MORE TIPS

Most shops are open Tuesday to Saturday from 9am or 10am until 6pm, on Monday from 1pm until 6pm, on Thursday until 9pm. Many shops open 12–5pm on Sunday, too. Cash is the normal method of payment, although credit cards are accepted at nearly all department stores and most of the larger shops. If you want to browse in the smaller shops it is customary to greet the owner who will be only too happy for you to look around.

selling herbs, spices and homeopathic remedies since 1743. All earthenware jars and 19th-century drawers full of aromatherapy remedies and health foods.
⊞ G5 **✉** Kloveniersburgwal 10–12 **☎** 624 3041 **🚇** Nieuwmarkt

JORRIT HEINEN
www.jorritheinen.com
Miniature ceramic canal houses, dolls in traditional costume, ornately decorated wooden boxes and trays. Also antique Delftware, royal and Makkum pottery and traditional tiles.
⊞ F6 **✉** Muntplein 12 **☎** 623 2271 **🚊** Tram 4, 9, 14, 16, 24, 25

MAISON DE BONNETERIE
www.debonneterie.nl
A gracious department store, popular with wealthy ladies.
⊞ F5 **✉** Rokin 140–142 **☎** 531 3400 **🚊** Tram 4, 9, 14, 16, 24, 25

METZ&CO
www.metz-co.com
Expensive gifts and designer funiture housed in a stylish department store. There is a café on the top floor.
⊞ F6 **✉** Leidsestraat 34–36 **☎** 520 7020 **🚊** Tram 1, 2, 5

NIC NIC
www.nicnicdesign.com
Irresistible knickknacks shop selling 1950s to 1970s collectibles and

near-antiques, all in good condition.

➕ E5
✉ Gasthuismolensteeg 5
☎ 622 8523 🚊 Tram 1, 2, 5

PALETTE

www.lesshoes.nl
What's said to be the smallest shop in the Netherlands has a large selection of silk and satin shoes, available in 500 different shades.

➕ F4 ✉ Nieuwezijds Voorburgwal 125 ☎ 639 3207 🚊 Tram 4, 9, 14, 16, 24, 25

P.G.C. HAJENIUS

www.hajenius.com
One of the world's finest tobacco shops, in elegant, art deco premises; in business for more than 250 years.

➕ F5 ✉ Rokin 92–96
☎ 623 7494 🚊 Tram 4, 9, 14, 16, 24, 25

PREMSELA & HAMBURGER

www.premsela.com
This refined setting for antique and contemporary silver and jewellery also does repair work.

➕ F5 ✉ Rokin 98 ☎ 624 9688 🚊 Tram 4, 9, 14, 16, 24, 25

SELEXYZ SCHELTEMA

www.selexyz.nl
The city's biggest bookshop, with a floor of computer software and audio and video titles.

➕ E6 ✉ Koningsplein 20
☎ 523 1411 🚊 Tram 1, 2, 5

DE SLEGTE

www.deslegte.com
Amsterdam's largest secondhand bookshop is good for bargains.

➕ F5 ✉ Kalverstraat 48–52
☎ 622 5933 🚊 Tram 4, 9, 14, 16, 24, 25

TAFT-OSCAR

www.taft.nl
Outrageous footwear and popular brand names like New Rock, Destroy and Sancho.

➕ F4 ✉ Nieuwendijk 208–10 ☎ 625 3143
🚊 Tram 4, 9, 14, 16, 24, 25

VITALS VITAMIN-ADVICE SHOP

www.vitaminadviceshop.nl
Vitamins and other food supplements, plus a computerized test that suggests supplements based on age and lifestyle.

➕ F4 ✉ Nieuwe Nieuwstraat 47 ☎ 427 4747
🚊 Tram 1, 2, 5, 13, 17

BARGAINS

There are often excellent bargains to be found in Amsterdam, especially during the January and July sales. Keep an eye out for signs saying *uitverkoop* (closing-down or end-of-season sale), *solden* (sale) and *korting* (discounted goods). On shop windows you may see *totaal uitverkoop* (clearance) when a shop is changing its lines for the new season or is closing down.

VROOM & DREESMANN

www.vd.nl
Clothing, jewellery, perfumes, electronics, leather goods, watches, clothing for the family and household goods all at reasonable prices.

➕ F5 ✉ Kalverstraat 203
☎ 0900 235 8363 (premium rate) 🚊 Tram 4, 9, 14, 16, 20, 24, 25

WATERSTONE'S

www.waterstones.com
Reliable English-language bookshop plus English newspapers and magazines and good guidebooks selection.

➕ F5 ✉ Kalverstraat 152
☎ 638 3821 🚊 1, 2, 4, 5, 9, 14, 16, 24, 25

WEBER'S HOLLAND

www.webersholland.nl
Fantastical and occasionally straight-out bizarre clothing and accessories, in the historic setting of the Klein Trippenhuis.

➕ G5 ✉ Kloveniersburgwal 26 ☎ 638 1777
🚇 Nieuwmarkt

WONDERWOOD

www.wonderwood.nl
A combination of shop and gallery, this is all about vintage plywood design from the 1940s to 1960s. The shop features more than 100 vintage plywood design chairs and re-editions are for sale.

➕ F5 ✉ Rusland 3 ☎ 625 3738 🚊 Tram 4, 9, 14, 16, 24, 25

Entertainment and Nightlife

AKHNATON
www.akhnaton.nl
Funky multicultural youth venue with reggae, rap and salsa dance nights. Be prepared for close dancing—this place gets full.
⊞ F4 ⊠ Nieuwezijds Kolk 25 ☎ 624 3396 ▣ Tram 1, 2, 5, 13, 17

AMSTERDAMS MARIONETTEN THEATER
www.marionettentheater.nl
Traditional puppet shows can be seen in this former blacksmith's. Opera is its specialty.
⊞ G4 ⊠ Nieuwe Jonkerstraat 8 ☎ 620 8027 ◎ Nieuwmarkt

ARC
www.bararc.eu
Great atmosphere at this recently opened classy cocktail bar and restaurant for straight and gay alike. Open every day from 10am, there is music and dancing until the early hours.
⊞ F6
⊠ Reguliersdwarsstraat 44 ☎ 689 7070 ▣ Tram 1, 2, 5

DE BEIAARD
www.beiaardgroep.nl
A beer drinker's paradise—over 80 beers from around the world.
⊞ E5 ⊠ Spui 30 ☎ 622 5110 ▣ Tram 1, 2, 5

BEURS VAN BERLAGE
www.beursvanberlage.nl
Home to the Netherlands Philharmonic Orchestra and Dutch Chamber Orchestra, this remarkable early modernist building, that once housed the stock exchange, makes an impressive concert hall.
⊞ F4 ⊠ Damrak 243 ☎ 530 4141 ▣ Tram 4, 9, 14, 16, 24, 25

CAFÉ DANTE
A good choice if you want to be with the young, good-looking crowd.
⊞ E5 ⊠ Spuistraat 320 ☎ 638 8839 ▣ Tram 1, 2, 5

DANSEN BIJ JANSEN
www.dansenbijjansen.nl
Student disco playing the latest chart toppers. You need student ID or be with a student, to get in.
⊞ E3 ⊠ Handboogstraat 11 ☎ 620 1779 ▣ Tram 1, 2, 5

BAR TALK

Most of the hundreds of bars and cafés in Amsterdam are open from around 10am until the early hours and many serve meals. *Proeflokalen* (tasting houses) open from around 4pm, and some serve snacks, such as nuts, cheese, meatballs and sausage. Beer is the most popular alcoholic drink. It is always served with a head, and often with a *jenever* chaser called a *kopstoot* (a blow to the head). If you want only a small beer, ask for a *colatje* or *kleintjepils*. Belgian beers are increasingly popular in Holland, and are considered more of a craft product.

DE DRIE FLESCHJES
Locals have been tasting gins at the Three Little Bottles since 1650.
⊞ F4 ⊠ Gravenstraat 18 ☎ 624 8443 ▣ Tram 1, 2, 4, 5, 9, 13, 14, 16, 17, 24, 25

DE DUIVEL
www.deduivel.nl
De Duivel was the city's first hip-hop club when it opened in 1992, and it's still popular today. Open until 3 to 4am Thursday to Saturday. Wednesday is open-mic night.
⊞ F6 ⊠ Reguliersdwarsstraat 87 ☎ 626 6184 ▣ Tram 4, 9, 16, 24, 25

DE ENGEL-BEWAARDER
Jazz on Sunday from 4pm livens up a usually tranquil, arty hangout just off the Red Light District.
⊞ F5 ⊠ Kloveniersburgwal 59 ☎ 625 3772 ◎ Nieuwmarkt

ENGELSE KERK
www.ercadam.nl
A chance to hear some excellent weekly baroque and choral concerts in tranquil surroundings.
⊞ E5 ⊠ Begijnhof 48 ☎ 624 9665 ▣ Tram 1, 2, 4, 5, 9, 14, 16, 24, 25

DE HEEREN VAN AEMSTEL
www.deheerenvanaemstel.nl
Prior to events such as Rotterdam's North Sea Jazz Festival, you can often see some of the world's great jazz performers here.

☎ 620 2173 🚊 Tram 4, 9, 14

HOPPE
www.café-hoppe.nl
One the most established, most popular brown cafés, with beer in one bar and gin from the barrel in another.
⊞ E5 ✉ Spui 18–20
☎ 420 4420 🚊 Tram 1, 2, 5

DE JAREN
www.café-de-jaren.nl
A spacious, ultramodern café, known for its trendy clientele. Sunny terraces overlooking the Amstel.
⊞ F5 ✉ Nieuwe Doelenstraat 20–22 ☎ 625 5771 🚊 Tram 4, 9, 14, 16, 24, 25

NIEUWE KERK
www.nieuwekerk.nl
Frequent lunchtime and evening concerts and exceptional organ recitals by visiting organists (▷ 46).
⊞ F4 ✉ Dam ☎ 638 6909 🚊 Tram 1, 2, 4, 5, 9, 13, 14, 16, 17, 24, 25

ODEON
www.odeontheater.nl
A converted canal house with house music playing on the first floor, classic disco from the 1960s to 1980s upstairs and jazz in the basement.
⊞ F6 ✉ Singel 460 ☎ 521 8555 🚊 Tram 1, 2, 5

DE OOIEVAAR
A homey atmosphere pervades the Stork, one of Holland's smallest *proeflokalen*.

⊞ G4 ✉ Sint-Olofspoort 1
☎ 625 7360 🚊 1, 2, 4, 5, 9, 13, 16, 17, 24, 25, 26

O'REILLY'S IRISH PUB
www.oreillys.com
Choice whiskeys and hearty Irish fare are accompanied by jolly folk music with a warm and friendly welcome.
⊞ E5 ✉ Paleisstraat 103–105
☎ 624 9498 🚊 Tram 1, 2, 5

OUDE KERK
www.oudekerk.nl
Chamber music concerts and organ recitals are held in this old church, where Holland's foremost composer, Jan Pieterszoon Sweelinck (1562–1621) was organist. Pass by at 4pm on Saturday, and you may hear a carillon concert (▷ 48).
⊞ G4 ✉ Oudekerksplein 23
☎ 625 8284 Ⓜ Nieuwmark
🚊 Tram 4, 9, 14, 24, 25

'DUTCH COURAGE'

Dutch gin (*jenever*), made from molasses and laced with juniper berries, comes in a variety of ages: *jong* (young), *oud* (old) and *zeer oud* (the oldest and the mellowest), and in shades ranging from clear to brownish. Other interesting tastes may be added; try *bessenjenever* (blackcurrant), or *bitterkoekjes likeur* (macaroon). *Jenever* is drunk straight or as a beer chaser, not with a mixer. Dutch for cheers is *Proost!*

PATHÉ TUSCHINSKI
www.pathe.nl/tuschinski
Holland's most attractive and prestigious cinema, with six screens. The classic art deco interior alone makes it worth visiting, no matter what's showing.
⊞ F6 ✉ Reguliersbreestraat 26–34 ☎ 0900 1458 (premium rate) 🚊 Tram 4, 9, 14

SUPPERCLUB
www.supperclub.nl
Much more than a dining experience with silver plates, music, live cabaret and complete relaxation. Eat off your lap while reclining and take a massage between courses. Set aside four hours for the dinner. Anything goes here and it is not for the sensitive or prudish.
⊞ E5 ✉ Jonge Roelensteeg 21 ☎ 344 6400 🚊 Tram 1, 2, 4, 13, 14, 16, 17, 24, 25

WINSTON KINGDOM
www.winston.nl
Live rock music is the attraction most nights at this Red Light District club, bar and restaurant.
⊞ F4 ✉ Warmoesstraat 131
☎ 623 1380 🚊 Tram 4, 9, 14, 16, 24, 25

WYNAND FOCKINK
www.wynand-fockink.nl
Down a side alley, this 1679 *proeflokaal* serves 100 or so gins and liqueurs. If the weather is warm, seek out the courtyard garden.
⊞ F4 ✉ Pijlsteeg 31–43
☎ 639 2695 🚊 Tram 4, 9, 14, 16, 24, 25

ENTERTAINMENT AND NIGHTLIFE

Restaurants

PRICES

Prices are approximate, based on a 3-course meal for one person.
€€€ over €50
€€ €25–€50
€ under €25

1E KLAS (€€)

www.restaurant1eklas.nl
This café-restaurant (pronounced 'Eerste Klas') is on Platform 2B in the old first-class waiting rooms at Amsterdam's Centraal Station. Enjoy continental cuisine in the grand old style of steam travel.
🞣 G3 ✉ Centraal Station, Stationsplein 15, Centrum ☎ 625 0131 🕐 Daily 8.30am–11pm 🚊 Tram 1, 2, 4, 5, 9, 13, 16, 17, 24, 25, 26

ANEKA RASA (€€)

This airy modern restaurant offers numerous vegetarian dishes that include an all-vegetarian *rijsttafel*. The attentive friendly staff serve amid a tropical ambience.
🞣 G4 ✉ Warmoesstraat 25–29, Centrum ☎ 626 1560 🕐 Daily 5–10.30 🚊 1, 2, 4, 5, 9, 13, 16, 17, 24, 25, 26

AL ARGENTINO (€€)

www.alargentino.nl
Sizzling steaks and spare ribs in a wood-panel, jolly-gaucho setting that brings a taste of the South American pampas to Amsterdam.
🞣 E5 ✉ Spui 3, Centrum ☎ 625 6764 🕐 Daily 11am–midnight 🚊 Tram 4, 9, 14, 16, 24

DE BRAKKE GROND (€–€€)

www.brasseriedebrakke grond.nl
The Flemish Cultural Centre's darkly atmospheric restaurant with a spacious terrace, serving bountiful portions of Belgian food. There is a great choice of Belgian beers to complement your meal.
🞣 F5 ✉ Nes 43, Centrum ☎ 626 0044 🕐 Mon–Thu 11am–1am, Fri, Sat 11am–2am, Sun noon–1am 🚊 Tram 4, 9, 14, 16, 24, 25

BRASSERIE DE POORT (€€)

Since 1870, this famous brasserie has sold more than 6 million numbered steaks. Every thousandth

COFFEE SHOPS

In Amsterdam, the expression 'coffee shop' refers to the 'smoking' coffee shops, where mostly young people hang out, high on hash. 'Smoking' coffee shops are usually easily recognizable by their psychedelic decor, thick fog of bitter smoke and mellow clientele. The cake on sale is sure to be drug-laced 'space cake'. Surprisingly, many such shops do a good cup of coffee. For just coffee you need to look out for a straightforward café or *kaffehuis*.

lucky diner gets a free bottle of house wine.
🞣 F4 ✉ Hotel Die Port van Cleve, Nieuwezijds Voorburgwal 176, Centrum ☎ 622 6429 🕐 Daily 7am–10.30pm 🚊 Tram 1, 2, 5, 13, 17

BRIDGES (€€€)

www.thegrand.nl
Fine French cuisine in an art nouveau setting, overlooked by a Karel Appel mural.
🞣 F4 ✉ Grand Hotel, Oudezijds Voorburgwal 197, Centrum ☎ 555 3111 🕐 Daily 6.30pm–11 🚇 Nieuwmarkt 🚊 Tram 4, 9, 14, 16, 24, 25

CAFÉ LUXEMBOURG (€–€€)

www.luxembourg.nl
Watch the world go by over canapés or club sandwiches on the terrace of this grand café.
🞣 E5 ✉ Spuistraat 24, Centrum ☎ 620 6264 🕐 Sun–Fri 9am–1am, Fri–Sat 9am–2am 🚊 Tram 1, 2, 5

CAFÉ PACIFICO (€)

www.cafépacifico.nl
The most authentic Mexican *bodega* in town. It gets especially crowded on Tuesday, which is margarita night when everyone is partying.
🞣 G4 ✉ Warmoesstraat 31, Centrum ☎ 624 2911 🕐 Sun–Thu 5–10.30, Fri–Sat 5–11 🚇 Centraal Station

CAFFE ESPRIT (€)

www.caffeesprit.nl
Designer café, all glass

and aluminium, run by the clothing chain next door. Sandwiches, salads, burgers and bagels. Sit outside in fine weather.
➕ E5 ✉ Spui 10, Centrum ☎ 622 1967 🕐 Sun–Fri 10–6 (Thu until 8), Sat 10–7 🚋 Tram 1, 2, 4, 5, 9, 14, 16, 24, 25

CHEZ GEORGES (€€€)

Belgian cuisine is widely considered to be more artisanal than Dutch—and besides, the portions are bigger. Georges affords evidence for both propositions, with fine dining in a candlelight setting.
➕ E4 ✉ Herenstraat 3, Grachtengordel ☎ 626 3332 🕐 Mon–Sat 6pm–11 🚋 Tram 1, 2, 5, 13, 17

DYNASTY (€€€)

www.restaurantdynasty.nl
A sophisticated and sumptuously decorated garden restaurant with fine Southeast Asian cuisine.
➕ F6 ✉ Reguliersdwarsstraat 30, Centrum ☎ 626 8400 🕐 Wed–Mon 5.30–10.30 🚋 Tram 1, 2, 5

EXCELSIOR (€€€)

www.leurope.nl
The formal restaurant of the Hôtel de l'Europe, overlooking the River Amstel, has top-flight continental cuisine and plush good looks.
➕ F5 ✉ Nieuwe Doelenstraat 2–8, Centrum ☎ 531 1705 🕐 Daily 7–11, 12.30–2.30 (except Sat, Sun), 7–10.30 🚋 4, 9, 14, 16, 24, 25

FROMAGERIE CRIGNON CULINAIR (€€)

Rustic French restaurant with eight different types of cheese fondue.
➕ F4 ✉ Gravenstraat 28, Centrum ☎ 624 6428 🕐 Tue–Sat 6pm–9.30pm 🚋 Tram 4, 9, 14, 16, 24, 25

GREENWOOD'S (€)

Little English-style tearoom serving scones with jam and cream, chocolate cake and lemon-meringue pie. Sit outside in summer.
➕ F4 ✉ Singel 103, Grachtengordel ☎ 623 7071 🕐 Daily 9.30–7 🚋 Tram 1, 2, 5, 13, 17

HAESJE CLAES (€€)

www.haesjeclaes.nl
Dutch cuisine at its best, served in a maze of wood panelled dining rooms in a building dating from the 16th-century.

➕ E5 ✉ Spuistraat 273–275, Centrum ☎ 624 9998 🕐 Daily 12–10pm 🚋 Tram 1, 2, 5

IN DE WAAG (€€)

www.indewaag.nl
You choose from an international menu, and eat at long, candlelit tables in a convivial space inside a medieval city gate and weigh house.
➕ G4 ✉ Nieuwmarkt 4, Centrum ☎ 422 7772 🕐 Daily 10am–1am Ⓜ Nieuwmarkt

KANTJIL & DE TIJGER (€€)

www.kantjil.nl
Modern decor and spicy, imaginative Javanese cuisine. Try the delicious *Nasi Rames*, a mini-*rijsttafel* on one plate.
➕ E5 ✉ Spuistraat 291–293, Centrum ☎ 620 0994 🕐 Daily 4.30–11 🚋 Tram 1, 2, 5

HET KARBEEL (€–€€)

www.hetkarbeel.nl
A café/restaurant serving everything from hearty breakfasts and lunches to filling full meals in pleasant surroundings..
➕ G4 ✉ Warmoesstraat 16, Centrum ☎ 627 4995 🕐 Daily 9.30am–11pm 🚋 1, 2, 4, 5, 9, 13, 16, 17, 24, 25, 26

KEUKEN VAN 1870 (€)

www.keukenvan1870.nl
This one-time soup kitchen, a shade gentrified, serves wholesome and hearty Dutch fare for a modest price.

🔲 F3 ✉ Spuistraat 4, Centrum ☎ 620 4018 🕐 Mon–Sat 5pm–10pm 🚊 Tram 1, 2, 5, 13, 17

LATEI (€)

www.latei.net

If you like couscous then head to this little vegetarian place on Thursday, Friday or Saturday night when a dinner menu is added to the daily fare of salads, soups, teas and tasty cakes.

🔲 G4 ✉ Zeedijk 143, Centrum ☎ 625 7485 🕐 Mon–Wed 8–6, Thu–Fri 8–10, Sat 9–10, Sun 11–6 🚇 Nieuwmarkt 🚊 Tram 4, 9, 14, 16, 24, 25

MEMORIES OF INDIA (€€)

www.memoriesofindia.nl

Tandoori, Moghlai and vegetarian cuisine in a refined colonial setting.

🔲 F6 ✉ Reguliersdwarsstraat 88, Centrum ☎ 623 5710 🕐 Daily 5pm–11.30pm 🚊 Tram 4, 9, 14, 16, 24, 25

MORITA-YA (€)

This traditional Japanese snack bar has very basic decor but serves great sushi and sashimi that won't break the bank.

🔲 G4 ✉ Zeedijk 18, Centrum ☎ 638 0756 🕐 Tue–Sun 6pm–10pm 🚊 1, 2, 4, 5, 9, 13, 16, 17, 24, 25, 26

NEW DORRIUS (€€€)

www.newdorrius.nl

A sophisticated take on the rustic Dutch style. Try the pike and cod delicacies, or cheese soufflé.

🔲 F4 ✉ Crowne Plaza Hotel, Nieuwezijds Voorburgwal 5, Centrum ☎ 420 2224 🕐 Daily 6.30am–11pm 🚊 Tram 1, 2, 5, 13, 17

OCHO LATIN GRILL (€€–€€€)

www.ochogrill.nl

A stylish restaurant that offers some of the best grilled food in town. High-quality beef raised on the South American pampas is a popular choice. If red meat is not for you, try the excellent chicken, fish, salads and fajitas.

🔲 F6 ✉ Reguliersdwarsstraat 8, Centrum ☎ 625 0592 🕐 Daily 4.30pm–11pm 🚊 Tram 1, 2, 5

LE PECHEUR (€€€)

www.lepecheur.nl

A smart fish-bistro with a secluded garden. Outstanding fresh oysters, caviar, sashimi and succulent lobster.

RIJSTTAFEL

The *rijsttafel* ('rice table') originally referred to the long list of ingredients required to prepare such a feast. It originated in early colonial days among hungry Dutch planters who, not satisfied by the basic Indonesian meal of rice and vegetables accompanied by meat or fish, always added other dishes. Thus the *rijsttafel* was born, a meal that ranges from a 6- to 10-item mini-*rijsttafel* to a 20- to 30-dish feast.

🔲 F6 ✉ Reguliersdwarsstraat 32, Centrum ☎ 624 3121 🕐 Closed Sat lunch and all day Sun 🚊 Tram 1, 2, 5

PIER 10 (€€)

www.pier10.nl

Dine on French-based international cuisine while enjoying the harbour views from a former 1930s shipping office behind Centraal Station.

🔲 G3 ✉ De Ruijterkade Steiger 10, Centrum ☎ 427 2310 🕐 Daily 6.30pm–midnight 🚊 1, 2, 4, 5, 9, 13, 16, 17, 24, 25, 26

DE ROODE LEEUW (€€)

www.hotelamsterdam.nl

The brasserie-style Red Lion serves up good stews and sauerkraut dishes.

🔲 F4 ✉ Hotel Amsterdam, Damrak 93–94, Centrum ☎ 555 0666 🕐 Daily 12–10 🚊 Tram 4, 9, 14, 16, 24, 25

ROSE'S CANTINA (€€)

www.rosescantina.com

Good value Tex-Mex meals in lively surroundings—probably the city's most popular restaurant.

🔲 F6 ✉ Reguliersdwarsstraat 40, Centrum ☎ 625 9797 🕐 Tue–Sun 5pm–11.30pm 🚊 Tram 4, 9, 14, 16, 24, 25

LA RUCHE (€)

www.debijenkorf.nl

Treat yourself to waffles with strawberries and cream in this café in De Bijenkorf department store (▷ 55), overlooking the Dam.

🔲 F4 ✉ Dam 1, Centrum

☎ 552 1772 🕙 Mon–Wed 11.30–6.30, Thu–Fri 11.30–8.30, Sat–Sun 11.30–5.30 🚊 Tram 4, 9, 14, 16, 24, 25

SAHID JAYA (€€)
www.ahidjaya.nl
A good choice for Indonesian-food newbies, because the fieriest spices have been used with relative moderation. The shady courtyard garden is especially nice to eat in during summer.
➕ F6 ✉ Reguliersdwarsstraat 26, Centrum ☎ 626 3727 🕙 Daily 5–11 🚊 Tram 1, 2, 5

SARANG MAS (€€)
www.sarangmas.eu
Modern surroundings counterpoint traditional cuisine. Well known for its authentic *rijsttafel* (rice tables, ▷ 63).
➕ F5 ✉ Rokin 84, Centrum ☎ 528 9590 🕙 Daily 11.30–11 🚊 Tram 4, 9, 14, 16, 24, 25

SHIBLI (€€€)
www.shibli.nl
Sit on a couch, as if inside a Bedouin tent, amid traditional ornaments, rugs and shishas, (waterpipes), dining on an Arabian banquet.
➕ F5 ✉ Oudezijds Voorburgwal 236 ☎ 554 6079 🕙 Daily 7pm–midnight 🚊 Tram 4, 9, 14, 16, 20, 24, 25

DE SILVEREN SPIEGEL (€€€)
www.desilverenspiegel.com
An exquisite classic

menu, complemented by one of the city's best wine lists, in a superbly restored 1614 house.
➕ F3 ✉ Kattengat 4–6, Centrum ☎ 624 6589 🕙 Daily 5.30pm–10.30pm 🚊 Tram 1, 2, 5, 13, 17

TANGO (€€)
www.tangorestaurant.nl
Small, authentic Buenos Aires-style Argentinian restaurant, with candlelight, on the edge of the Red Light District. Try the juicy steaks.
➕ F4 ✉ Warmoesstraat 49, Centrum ☎ 627 2467 🕙 Daily 5–11.30 🚊 Tram 4, 9, 14, 16, 24, 25

TEPPANYAKI NIPPON (€€–€€€)
www.teppanyakinippon.nl
One of Holland's first ever Japanese grill restaurants keeps the flame burning bright in a

TIPPING

Most restaurant windows display menus giving the price of individual dishes including BTW (value-added tax) and a 15 per cent service charge. You don't really need to worry too much about tipping but nevertheless, most Amsterdammers leave a small tip or round up the bill (check). This tip should be left as change rather than included on a credit card payment. If you feel you have good service then that's the time to leave a tip.

chic dining room that has a sushi bar too.
➕ F6 ✉ Reguliersdwarsstraat 18–20, Centrum ☎ 620 8787 🕙 Daily 6pm–11.30pm 🚊 Tram 4, 9, 14, 16, 24, 25

TOKYO CAFÉ (€€)
www.tokyocafé.nl
Excellent sushi and sashimi in the Japanese café, and a range of *teppanyaki* dinner menus from the simple to the stunning, with lobster soup and king prawns.
➕ F5 ✉ Spui 15, Centrum ☎ 489 7918 🕙 Daily 11–11 🚊 Tram 1, 2, 4, 5, 9, 14, 16, 24, 25

TUYNHUYS (€€€)
www.tuynhuys.nl
Sophisticated French-style cuisine using mostly local ingredients. The Tuynhuys is in a converted coach house and garden.
➕ F6 ✉ Reguliersdwarsstraat 28, Centrum ☎ 627 6603 🕙 Daily 6pm–10.30pm (also Mon–Fri noon–2.30) 🚊 Tram 4, 9, 14, 16, 24, 25

D'VIJFF VLIEGHEN (€€–€€€)
www.thefiveflies.com
The menu in the Five Flies, in five 17th-century houses, has an impressive collection of 'New Dutch' dishes, imaginative and beautifully presented. The set meal is good value. You might even sit next to a Rembrandt etching.
➕ F5 ✉ Spuistraat 294–302, Centrum ☎ 530 4060 🕙 Daily 6pm–10pm 🚊 Tram 1, 2, 5

The district lying to the east of the hub of the city has a different feel. Here you are away from the tourists, with residential housing and modern development set within the canals and docks.

Joods Historisch Museum

Silver Hanukkah lamp (left) on display at the Jewish Historical Museum (right)

HIGHLIGHTS

● Grote Synagoge (Great Synagogue, 1671)
● Holy Ark (1791)
● Haggadah Manuscript (1734)

DID YOU KNOW?

● 1597–The first Jew gained Dutch citizenship.
● 102,000 of the 140,000-strong Dutch Jewish community were exterminated in World War II.

A remarkable exhibition devoted to Judaism and the story of Jewish settlement in Amsterdam. The most memorable and poignant part portrays the horrors of the Holocaust.

Reconstruction In the heart of what used to be a Jewish area, this complex of four former synagogues forms the largest and most important Jewish museum outside Israel. The buildings lay in ruins for many years after World War II and were later restored. The quartet of historical synagogues is a site well worth exploring.

Historical exhibits The New Synagogue (1752) gives a lengthy, detailed history of Zionism, with displays of religious objects. The Great Synagogue (1671), of more general interest, defines the role of the Jewish community in Amsterdam's trade and industry. Downstairs is a chilling exhibition from the war years and a moving collection by Jewish painters. The remaining two synagogues in the complex are the Obbene Sjoel (1685) and the Dritt Sjoel (1778).

The Dockworker The Nazis occupied Amsterdam in May 1940 and immediately began to persecute the Jewish population. In February 1941, 400 Jews were gathered outside the Great Synagogue by the SS, herded into trucks and taken away. This triggered the February Strike, a general strike led by dockers. Though suppressed after only two days, it was Amsterdam's first open revolt against Nazism and gave impetus to the resistance movement.

The Magere Brug or Skinny Bridge looks attractive illuminated at night

Magere Brug

This traditional double-leaf Dutch drawbridge is a city landmark, and one of the most photographed sights in Amsterdam at night, illuminated by strings of enchanting lights.

Skinny sisters Of Amsterdam's 1,200 or so bridges, the wooden 'Skinny Bridge' is, without doubt, the best known. On the Amstel river, it is a 20th-century replica of a 17th-century drawbridge. Tradition has it that, in 1670, a simple footbridge was built by two elderly sisters named Mager (meaning skinny), who lived on one side of the Amstel and wanted easy access to their carriage and horses, stabled on the other bank. It seems more likely, however, that the bridge took its name from its narrow girth. In 1772 it was widened and became a double drawbridge, enabling ships of heavy tonnage to sail up the Amstel from the IJ, an inlet of what was then a sea called the Zuiderzee and is today the IJsselmeer, a freshwater lake.

City uproar In 1929 the city council started discussing whether to demolish the old frame, which had rotted. It was to be replaced with an electrically operated bridge. After a huge outcry, the people of Amsterdam voted overwhelmingly to save the original wooden bridge.

Latest crossing The present bridge, made of African azobe wood, was erected in 1969 and its mechanical drive installed in 1994. Its graceful proportions are still pleasing to the eye.

THE BASICS

➕ G6
✉ At Kerkstraat on the Amstel river
Ⓦ Waterlooplein
🚋 Tram 4

DID YOU KNOW?

● Around 63,000 boats pass under the bridge each year.
● The rebuilding of the bridge in 1969 cost €63,530.
● There are 60 drawbridges in Amsterdam; 8 are wooden.

THE EAST

TOP 25

Museum Het Rembrandthuis

Not always respected during his lifetime, Rembrandt's image and work is everywhere

THE BASICS

www.rembrandthuis.nl

🔲 G5

✉ Jodenbreestraat 4

☎ 520 0400

🕐 Daily 10–5. Closed 1 Jan

Ⓜ Nieuwmarkt, Waterlooplein

🚊 Tram 9, 14

🚢 Museum Boat North/ South Line stop 5; Golden Age Line stop 6

♿ Few

✋ Moderate

❓ Brief film of Rembrandt's life

HIGHLIGHTS

● *Self-portrait with a Surprised Expression*

● *Five Studies of the Head of Saskia* and one of *An Older Woman*

● *View of Amsterdam*

● *Christ Shown to the People*

The absence of Rembrandt's own belongings from this intimate house is more than compensated for by its collection of his etchings, which is virtually complete. They are fascinating.

From riches to rags In this red-shuttered canal house, Rembrandt spent the happiest and most successful years of his life, producing many of his most famous paintings and prints. Through his wife, the wealthy heiress Saskia van Uylenburgh, the up-and-coming young artist was introduced to Amsterdam's patrician class and commissions for portraits poured in. He rapidly became an esteemed painter, and bought this large house in 1639 as a symbol of his newfound respectability. Following Saskia's death, aged 30, in 1642 soon after the birth of their son Titus, Rembrandt's work became unfashionable. In 1656 he was declared bankrupt. The house and most of his possessions were sold in 1658, although Rembrandt continued to live here until 1660, when he was obliged to leave. He died a pauper in 1669.

Funny faces Rembrandt's achievements in etching (many created in this house) were as important as those in his painting, since his mastery in this medium inspired its recognition as an art form for the first time. Four of his copper etching plates are also on display, together with a series of biblical illustrations. Look out for Rembrandt's studies of street figures hung alongside some highly entertaining self-portraits in various guises, and some mirror-images of himself making faces.

Both inside and out, the Willet-Holthuysen museum oozes classical elegance

Museum Willet-Holthuysen

Behind the impressive facade of this beautifully preserved, gracious mansion lies a lavishly decorated, sumptuously furnished home with a delightful garden, a rare luxury in Amsterdam.

Insight Standing on Herengracht, Amsterdam's most elegant canal (▷ 44), this house was built in 1687 for Jacob Hop, a wealthy member of the city council. It changed hands many times and eventually, in 1855, came into the possession of a glass merchant named Pieter Gerard Holthuysen. On his death, it became the home of his daughter Sandra and her husband, the art collector Abraham Willet, who together built up a valuable collection of glass, silver, ceramics and paintings. The couple bequeathed the house and its contents to the city in 1895, to be used as a museum. For many years it was visited rarely. However, following extensive restoration in the late 1990s, the museum attracts an increasing number of visitors, and provides a rare insight into life in the grand canal-houses in the 17th to 19th centuries.

Luxury and grandeur The rooms are decorated with inlaid wood and lacquered panels with painted ceilings. Be sure to see the Blue Room, formerly the preserve of the gentlemen of the house, and the 17th-century kitchen, with its original plumbing. Guests would be served tea in the tiny, round Garden Room that, painted in the customary pale green, looks out over an immaculate French-style formal garden This rare 18th-century garden is a jewel not to be missed.

THE BASICS

www.willetholthuysen.nl
⊞ G6
⊠ Herengracht 605
☎ 523 1822
🕐 Mon–Fri 10–5, Sat–Sun and public hols 11–5.
Closed 1 Jan, 30 Apr, 25 Dec
🚇 Waterlooplein
🚊 Tram 4, 9, 14
⛴ Museum Boat North/South Line stop 5; Golden Age Line stop 6
♿ None
💷 Moderate

HIGHLIGHTS

● Blue Room
● Dining Room
● Porcelain and silver collections
● Kitchen
● Garden Room
● Garden

Nederlands Scheepvaartmuseum

HIGHLIGHTS

● The *Amsterdam*
● Royal sloop
● Blaeu's World Atlas
● First printed map of Amsterdam
● Three-masted ship
● Wartime exhibits

TIPS

● Check in advance if there are any special activities planned.
● Mind your head as you go around the ship unless you are below 1m (3ft 4in) tall.

Holland's glorious seafaring history gets due recognition at this museum, which displays with contemporary flair a fine collection of ships, full-size replicas, and models and artefacts.

Admiralty storehouse The vast neoclassical building (1656) that now houses the Maritime Museum was formerly the Dutch Admiralty's central store. Here the United East India Company (VOC) would load their ships prior to the eight-month journey to Jakarta, headquarters of the VOC in Indonesia. In 1973, the arsenal was converted into this museum, which has a large collection of ships.

Voyages of discovery An ancient dugout, a re-created section of a destroyer, luxury liners and

The delightful and superbly decorated stern of the replica of the Amsterdam, an 18th-century Dutch East Indiaman (left); Amsterdam's Maritime Museum's most popular exhibit is moored close to the building that houses a fascinating seafaring collection (right)

schooners depict Holland's remarkable maritime history. Peer through periscopes and operate a radar set, marvel at some 500 magnificent model ships and study the charts, instruments, weapons, and maps from the great age of exploration. Don't miss the first sea atlas, the mid-16th century three-masted ship model, or the fine royal sloop—the 'golden coach on water'—last used in 1962 for Queen Juliana's silver wedding anniversary.

The *Amsterdam* The highlight of the museum is the *Amsterdam*, a replica of an 18th-century Dutch East Indiaman that sank off the English coast in 1749 during her maiden voyage. A vivid film *Voyage to the East Indies* is shown, and in summer, actors become bawdy 'sailors', firing cannons, swabbing the decks, loading cargo and enacting burials at sea.

THE BASICS

www.scheepvaartmuseum.nl

+ J5

✉ Kattenburgerplein 1

☎ 523 2222

🕐 The museum has been closed for a renovation expected to be completed by summer 2011. During this time the *Amsterdam* can be visited at Science Center NEMO (▷ 77)

🚌 Bus 22, 42, 43

⛴ Museum Boat Golden Age Line, stop 2, 8

♿ Very good

💶 Expensive

73

More to See

AMSTEL

The river is a busy commercial thoroughfare, with barges carrying goods to and from the port. In town, its bustling banks are lined by houseboats.

➕ G6 🚊 Tram 3, 7, 9, 10, 12, 14

AMSTELKERK

Squat and wooden, this Calvinist church (1670) was originally meant to be a temporary structure.

➕ F7 ✉ Amstelveld 🕐 Closed except during 10.30am Sun service 🚊 Tram 4 🎟 Free

GROENBURGWAL

This picturesque canal near the Muziektheater was Monet's preferred choice.

➕ F5 🚇 Nieuwmarkt

HERMITAGE AMSTERDAM

www.hermitage.nl

Opened in the 17th-century Amstelhof complex as a 'branch' of St. Petersburg's Hermitage Museum. Changing exhibitions are taken from the Russian parent's collection of art, fine art and crafts.

➕ G6 ✉ Amstelhof, Amstel 51 ☎ 0900 437648243 🕐 Daily 10–5 (Wed to 8pm) 🚇 Waterlooplein 🚢 Museum Boat Golden Age Line, stop 5 🚊 Tram 9, 14 ♿ Very good 🎟 Expensive

HORTUS BOTANICUS

www.hortus-botanicus.nl

With more than 8,000 plant species, Amsterdam's oldest botanical garden (established in 1682) has one of the largest collections in the world. It has tropical greenhouses, a medicinal herb garden and an orchid nursery.

➕ H6 ✉ Plantage Middenlaan 2a ☎ 625 9021 🕐 Feb–end Nov Mon–Fri 9–5, Sat–Sun 10–5 (until 7 Jul–Aug); Dec–end Jan until 4 🍴 Café 🚊 Tram 9, 14 ♿ Good 🎟 Moderate

JODENBUURT

Jewish refugees first settled here in the 16th century. Almost the entire district was razed to the ground at the end of World War II, leaving only a few synagogues (▷ 68), mansions and diamond factories as legacy of a once-thriving community.

➕ G5 🚇 Waterlooplein

Palm house, Hortus Botanicus (left)
Boats moored on the Amstel river (above)
Zuiderkerk seen from picturesque Groenburgwal

MUSEUM VAN LOON

www.museumvanloon.nl

The Van Loon family lived in this house during the 19th century holding important positions as city mayors and in the United East India Company. The house and its collection are in fine condition, as is the garden.

➕ F6 ✉ Keizersgracht 672 ☎ 624 5255 ⏱ Wed–Mon 11–5 🚊 Tram 16, 24, 25 ✋ Moderate

MUZIEKTHEATER

www.hetmuziektheather.nl

Amsterdam's venue for opera and dance is affectionately known as the 'false teeth' because of its white marble panelling and redbrick roof. The complex includes the buildings of the new town hall (Stadhuis). The design caused great controversy when it was built in 1986, and its construction in the heart of an 'alternative' zone sparked riots.

➕ G5 ✉ Waterlooplein 22 ☎ 551 8117 or 551 8006 (recorded information) Ⓜ Waterlooplein 🚊 Tram 9, 14

NATIONAAL VAKBONDSMUSEUM

It is really the building that is of most interest as the museum devoted to trade unions is perhaps not the most appealing of subjects. The exterior is impressive and its grandiose interior full of designs by leading artists of the day. Sunlight streams through a double roof of yellow and white glass.

➕ H5 ✉ Henri Polaklaan 9 ☎ 624 1166 ⏱ Tue–Fri 11–5, Sun 1–5 (check as museum reopens in 2010 after refurbishment) 🚊 Tram 9 ♿ Good ✋ Inexpensive

PORTUGESE SYNAGOGE

www.esnoga.com

Holland's finest synagogue, one of the first of any size in Western Europe. It is remarkable that this imposing building escaped destruction in World War II.

➕ G6 ✉ Mr Visserplein 3 ☎ 624 5351 ⏱ Nov–end Mar Sun–Thu 10–4, Fri 10–2; Apr–end Oct Sun–Fri 10–4; service on Sat at 9am. Closed Jewish hols, Sun 10–12 Ⓜ Waterlooplein 🚢 Museum Boat North/South Line stop 5; Golden Age Line stop 6 🚊 Tram 9, 14 ✋ Moderate

Muziektheater–home to ballet and opera

The copper hull of Science Center NEMO

REGULIERSGRACHT
Seven bridges cross the water here.
Tour boats slow to give you a view
of the identical humped bridges
stretching along the canal. With their
strings of lights, they are best viewed
from the water at night.
➕ F6 🚊 Tram 4, 16, 24, 25

SCHEEPVAARTHUIS
The peculiarly tapered Maritime House,
suggests the bow of an approaching
ship. Commissioned in 1912, it
represents an impressive example of
Amsterdam School architecture.
➕ G4 ✉ Prins Hendrikkade 108–111
🚌 Bus 22, 42, 43

SCIENCE CENTER NEMO
www.e-nemo.nl
Children are likely to enjoy learning at
this impressive hands-on, interactive
museum of modern technology.
Loads of opportunities to experiment
and explore the worlds of science
and computing. The building itself is
striking, designed by Italian architect
Renzo Piano in 1997. Its crowning

glory is the roof terrace, a lovely place
to relax or watch the sunset.
➕ H4 ✉ Oosterdok 2 ☎ 531 3233
🕐 Tue–Sun 10–5 (also Mon Jun–end Aug)
🍴 Café 🚌 Bus 22, 42, 43 ⛴ Museum
Boat Golden Age Line, stop 2, 8 ♿ Very
good 💶 Expensive

TASSENMUSEUM HENDRIKJE
www.tassenmuseum.nl
A handbag (purse) museum might
not be on everyone's must-see list,
but this interesting collection has bags
dating from the 1500s to the latest
designer items, and is housed in a
graceful old canal house.
➕ F6 ✉ Herengracht 573 ☎ 524 6452
🕐 Daily 10–5 🚊 Tram 4, 9, 14

ZUIDERKERK
Holland's first Protestant church (1614)
is one of the city's most beautiful, with
an 80m (265ft) tower. Its designer,
Hendrick de Keyser, lies buried within.
➕ G5 ✉ Zuiderkerkhof 72 ☎ 552 7977
🕐 Mon–Fri 9–4, Sat 12–4; tower Jun–end Sep
Wed–Sat 2–4 Ⓜ Nieuwmarkt 💶 Free;
tower moderate

*The unusually shaped
Scheepvaarthuis building*

The soaring spire of Zuiderkerk

Shopping

THE EAST · SHOPPING

DE BEESTENWINKEL
www.beestenwinkel.nl
A cuddly toy shop for all ages. Ideal for collectors and small gifts.
➕ F5 ✉ Staalstraat 26
☎ 623 1805 🚃 Tram 9, 14

BLOEMEN-EN PLANTENMARKT
Although not as well known as the flower market on Singel (▷ 43), the weekly flower and plant market on this Prinsengracht square is more like a 'normal' market.
➕ F7 ✉ Amstelveld
🕐 Mon 9–6 🚃 Tram 4

CONCERTO
www.platomania.eu
Finest all-round selection of new and used records and CDs. Good for jazz, classical music and 1950s and 1960s hits.
➕ G6 ✉ Utrechtsestraat 52–60 ☎ 623 5228
🚃 Tram 4

EDUARD KRAMER
www.antique-tileshop.nl
A huge selection of old Dutch tiles, the earliest dating from the 1500s; many rescued from the kitchens of old canal houses. Also ornaments.
➕ E6 ✉ Nieuwe Spiegelstraat 64 ☎ 623 0832 🚃 Tram 7, 10

EPISODE
www.episode.eu
One of two branches in Amsterdam of a small chain that specializes in vintage fashion, aimed at alternative sensibilities on a tight budget.
➕ G5 ✉ Waterlooplein 1
☎ 320 3000 🚃 Tram 9, 14

GASSAN DIAMONDS
www.gassandiamonds.com
A tour (daily) of the diamond-polishing and cutting workshop that leads inevitably to the sales room.
➕ G5 ✉ Nieuwe Uilenburgerstraat 173–175
☎ 622 5333 🚇 Waterlooplein
🚃 Tram 9, 14

DE KLOMPENBOER
www.woodenshoefactory.com
Authentic clog factory with the city's largest selection of beautifully handcrafted footwear.
➕ G5 ✉ Sint-Antoniesbreestraat 39–51
☎ 623 0632 🚇 Nieuwmarkt

JASKI ART GALLERY
www.jaski.nl
The gallery specializes

GOING, GOING, GONE

Amsterdam's main auction houses are Sotheby's (✉ De Boelelaan 30 ☎ 550 2200) and Christie's (✉ Cornelis Schuytstraat 57 ☎ 575 5255). Their Dutch counterpart, Botterweg Auctions Amsterdam (☎ 777 5900). All hold presale viewings, interesting even if you have no intention of buying. Dutch school paintings are of course high on the agenda and special auctions are devoted to this subject.

in painting, sculpture, ceramics and graphic art by the CoBrA artists (1948–1951).
➕ E6 ✉ Nieuwe Spiegelstraat 29 ☎ 620 3939
🚃 Tram 7, 10

MODERN ART MARKET
Paintings, pottery and sculpture plus classical music or jazz at this elegant Sunday market.
➕ F6 ✉ Thorbeckeplein
🕐 Apr–Oct Sun 10.30–6
🚃 Tram 4, 9, 14

PATISSERIE HOLTKAMP
www.patisserieholtkamp.nl
An art deco storefront is the icing on the cake for a luscious array of patisserie—cakes, tarts, fruit pies, and more, including Dutch specialties.
➕ F7 ✉ Vijzelgracht 15
☎ 624 8757 🚃 Tram 7, 10, 16, 24, 25

PUCCINI BOMBONI
Delicious pralines handmade with fresh cream and a variety of fillings are the 'dangerous' specialism of this small store.
➕ G5 ✉ Stalstraat 17
☎ 626 5474 🚃 Tram 9, 14

WATERLOOPLEIN-MARKT
Amsterdam's liveliest market is full of funky clothes, curiosities, 'antique' junk and more.
➕ G5 ✉ Waterlooplein
🕐 Mon–Fri 9–5, Sat 8.30–5.30 🚇 Waterlooplein
🚃 Tram 9, 14

Entertainment and Nightlife

CAFÉ DE SLUYSWACHT
www.sluyswacht.nl
The rickety 17th-century Sluyswacht building is right on the canal. There are tables outside and a cosy inside bar with wooden tables and beams that is full until the early hours.
🔢 G5 ✉ Jodenbreestraat 1 ☎ 625 7611 ⏰ Daily 11.30am–1am (Fri–Sat 3am) 🚇 Waterlooplein 🚊 Tram 9, 14

CAFÉ HOOGHOUDT
www.hooghoudtamsterdam.nl
This brown bar-cum-*proeflokaal* is lined with stoneware *jenever* barrels. Tasty Dutch appetizers go with a big selection of liqueurs.
🔢 F6 ✉ Reguliersgracht 11 ☎ 420 4041 ⏰ Tue–Sat 4pm–12 🚊 Tram 4, 9, 14, 16, 24, 25

CAFÉ SCHILLER
An evocative art deco bar enhanced with live piano music. Sophisticated for Rembrandtplein.
🔢 F6 ✉ Rembrandtplein 24 ☎ 624 9846 🚊 Tram 4, 9, 14

CLUB HOME
www.clubhome.nl
Dress smartly for this club, with three floors each with different music. Free before midnight.
🔢 G6 ✉ Wagenstraat 3–7 ☎ 620 1375 ⏰ Thu–Sat from 11pm 🚊 Tram 4, 9, 14

ESCAPE
www.escape.nl
Amsterdam's largest dance club, which can hold 2,000 dancers, has a superb light show and sound system. The week's biggest draw is Framebusters on Saturday.
🔢 F6 ✉ Rembrandtplein 11 ☎ 622 1111 ⏰ 11pm–4am (Fri–Sat until 5am) 🚊 Tram 4, 9, 14

GREENHOUSE NAMASTE
www.greenhouse.org
Relaxing place to enjoy a smoke in one of the city's famous coffeeshops, with a tiny lounge at the back.
🔢 G6 ✉ Waterlooplein 345 ☎ 622 5499 ⏰ Daily 9am– 1am (Fri–Sat until 2am) 🚇 Waterlooplein 🚊 Tram 9, 14

KONINKLIJK THEATER CARRÉ
www.theatercarre.nl
The Royal Theatre hosts

FILM GUIDE
The city's main multiscreen cinema complexes, in the Leidseplein and Rembrandtplein areas, follow Hollywood's lead closely. The latest big US releases and British films that become international hits are sure to show up on Amsterdam's screens after a short delay. Films from other countries occasionally make it to the screen. Almost all films are shown in their original language, with Dutch subtitles; an important exception is children's films, which are largely screened in Dutch.

long-running international musicals, revues, cabaret, folk dancing and an annual Christmas circus.
🔢 G7 ✉ Amstel 115–25 ☎ 0900 252 5255 🚇 Weesperplein

DE KROON
www.dekroon.nl
This bar/café/dance club affects a cool, hard-edged modernity as if to belie a location on the rambunctious Rembrandtplein.
🔢 F6 ✉ Rembrandtplein 17 ☎ 625 2011 🚊 Tram 4, 9, 14

MUZIEKTHEATER
www.hetmuziektheater.nl
Home to the Nederlands Opera and the Nationale Ballet since it opened in 1986. The Netherland's largest auditorium, seating 1,689, mounts an international repertoire as well as experimental works from its resident companies, plus leading international companies. Guided backstage tours on Saturday at noon (▷ 76).
🔢 G6 ✉ Amstel 3 ☎ 551 8117 or 551 8006 (recorded information) 🚇 Waterlooplein 🚊 Tram 9, 14

RAIN
www.rain-amsterdam.com
Rain is a great combination of chic surroundings, good food, classy cocktails and late-night dancing to a blend of global sounds.
🔢 F6 ✉ Rembrandtplein 44 ☎ 626 7078 ⏰ Sun–Thu 6pm–2am, Fri, Sat 6pm–4am 🚊 Tram 4, 9, 14

Restaurants

PRICES

Prices are approximate, based on a 3-course meal for one person.

€€€   over €50
€€   €25–€50
€   under €25

BREITNER (€€–€€€)

www.restaurant-breitner.nl
Picture windows afford views of the Amstel and Herengracht, while inside, the French-based menu tracks the seasons and is open to global influences.
🔼 G6   ✉ Amstel 212, Grachtengordel   ☎ 627 7879
🕐 Mon–Sat 6pm–11pm
🚋 Tram 9, 14

CAFÉ DE FLES (€€)

www.defles.nl
Warm cellar full of large wooden tables. A real locals' hangout.
🔼 F6   ✉ Vijzelstraat 137, Grachtengordel (the entrance is via Prinsengracht 955)
☎ 624 9644   🕐 Daily 5pm–1am (Fri– Sat until 2)
🚋 Tram 16, 24, 25

GOLDEN TEMPLE (€)

www.restaurantgoldentemple.com
An imaginative menu of Indian, Mexican and Middle Eastern dishes.
🔼 G7   ✉ Utrechtsestraat 126, Grachtengordel   ☎ 626 8560   🕐 Daily 5pm–9.30pm
🚋 Tram 4

HEMELSE MODDER (€€)

www.hemelsenodder.nl
Sophisticated mains and delicious desserts.
🔼 G4   ✉ Oude Waal 11, Centrum   ☎ 624 3203
🕐 Tue–Sun 6pm–10pm
🚇 Nieuwmarkt

INDRAPURA (€€)

www.indrapura.nl
A popular colonial-style Indonesian restaurant. Tell the waiter how hot and spicy you want your dishes to be. Some of the best *rijsttafel* in town.
🔼 F6   ✉ Rembrandtplein 40-42, Rembrandtplein
☎ 623 7329   🕐 Daily 5pm–10pm   🚋 Tram 4, 9, 14

PINTO (€€)

www.pinto-restaurant.com
This restaurant in the Jewish quarter serves mainly kosher Israeli and French cuisine, plus sandwiches and take-out food.
🔼 G5   ✉ Jodenbreestraat 144, Centrum   ☎ 625 0923
🕐 Sun–Thu 12–10   🚋 Tram 9, 14

SEGUGIO (€€€)

www.segugio.nl
Romantic Italian that's

FISH AND VEGETABLES

Although the Dutch eat a lot of meat, Amsterdam with its seagoing associations has a great choice of fish restaurants. Vegetarians, too, have specialty eating places to suit all tastes and budgets, while others, most notably pizzerias and the Asian restaurants around town, offer separate sections in the menus for vegetarian dishes.

worth the splurge, with daily fish, risotto and soup specials, but leave room for the superb *zabaione* and a glass of grappa.
🔼 G7   ✉ Utrechtsestraat 96, Grachtengordel   ☎ 330 1503
🕐 Mon–Sat 6pm–11pm
🚋 Tram 4

STEAKHOUSE PIET DE LEEUW (€–€€)

www.pietdeleeuw.nl
Steaks, steaks and yet more steaks are the house specialty at this atmospheric old place, but there are also some traditional dishes.
🔼 F7   ✉ Noorderstraat 11, Grachtengordel   ☎ 623 7181
🕐 Mon–Fri 12–11, Sat–Sun 5pm–11pm   🚋 Tram 16, 24, 25

TEMPO DOELOE (€€)

www.tempodoeloerestaurant.nl
Indonesian restaurant, notable for its western interior, exotic flowers and some of the hottest dishes in town.
🔼 G6   ✉ Utrechtsestraat 75, Grachtengordel   ☎ 625 6718
🕐 Daily 6pm–11.30pm
🚋 Tram 4

LE ZINC... ET LES AUTRES (€€)

www.lezinc.nl
Home-style French cuisine in a converted canalside warehouse. Choose from two *prix-fixe* menus, one of which is the chef's surprise, plus a first-class *à la carte* menu.
🔼 F7   ✉ Prinsengracht 999, Grachtengordel   ☎ 622 9044
🕐 Mon–Sat 5.30pm–11pm
🚋 Tram 4

A distinct district set apart from the city's historic heart, close to the main city park. Not just a bland area of suburbia, but an important cultural area, with museums celebrating Amsterdam's best-known artists.

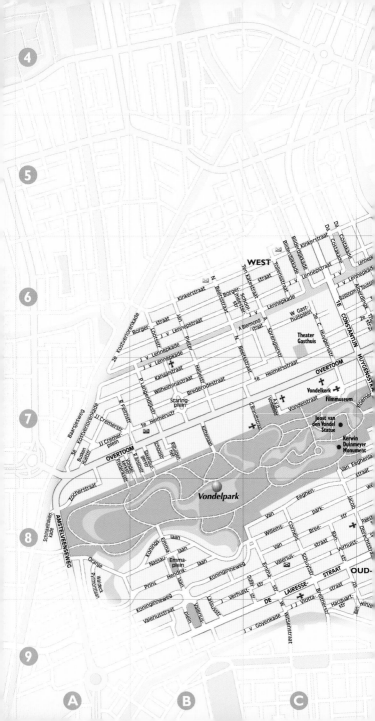

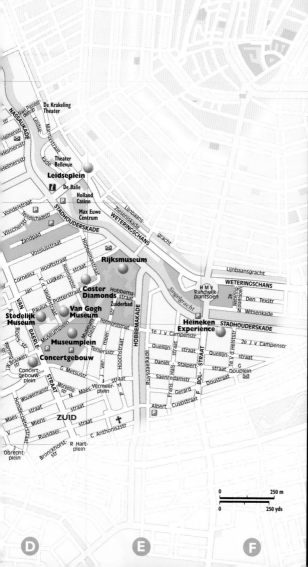

De Krakeling Theater

Nwe passeder dersstr

NASSAUKADE

Helmersstr
Helmersstr
Helmersstr

Marnixstraat

Leidse

Theater Bellevue

Leidseplein

De Balie

Holland Casino

Max Euwe Centrum

STADHOUDERSKADE

Vondelstraat

Testelschadestr

Zieseniskade

Lijnbaans.

WETERINGSCHANS

gracht

Visscherstr

Vossiusstraat

Zandpad

Hobbemastraat

Rijksmuseum

Lijnbaansgracht

Singelgracht

WETERINGSCHANS

2e Wetering plantsoen

Den Texstr

Hooftstraat

Cornelisz.

Jan Luijken str

straat

Coster Diamonds

Hobbemastraat

H M v Randwijk-plantsoen

N Witsenkade

Stedelijk Museum

P C Hooftstraat

Van Baerle

Paulus Potterstraat

Zuiderbad

Van Gogh Museum

Honthorststraat

HOBBEMAKADE

Heineken Experience

STADHOUDERSKADE

2e J v Campenstr

Boers str

Ruysdaelkade

Museumplein

Museum straat

1e J v Campenstr

Quellijn straat

Quellijnstr

2e J v Heisstr

Brouwers

VAN BAERLE

Concertgebouw

Teniersstr

Frans Hals straat

Stalpert

straat

G Douplein

Vermeerman

G. Metsustr

Vec

Daniel

Saenredamstr

Gerard

Doustraat

Concert-gebouw-plein

STRAAT

Wouwerman

Moreelse

Maes straat

straat

Vermeer-plein

Ferdinand

BOL STRAAT

Maes-dtkl

Miens str

Ruysdael-straat

ZUID

straat

Albert Cuypstraat

Ruysdael-dtkl str

V

C Anthoniszstr

Obrecht-plein

Bronckhorst-str

R Hart-plein

0   250 m

0   250 yds

Leidseplein

Amsterdam's liveliest square, Leidseplein, buzzes with life both by day and by night

THE BASICS

- E6
- Leidseplein
- Restaurants and cafés
- Tram 1, 2, 5, 7, 10
- Museum Boat North/South Line stop 3

HIGHLIGHTS

- American Hotel (1904)
- Stadsschouwburg (1894)
- Street entertainment

This square represents Amsterdam's nightlife at its most vibrant. It is filled with street cafés, ablaze with neon and abuzz with street entertainers.

Party district for centuries During the Middle Ages, farmers on their way to market unloaded their carts here, at the outskirts of the city. At the turn of the 19th century, artists and writers gathered here. In the 1930s Leidseplein was the site of many clashes between political factions, and it became the main site of anti-Nazi rallies during the war. In the 1960s it was the stomping ground of the *Pleiners* (Dutch Mods). Today, despite the constant flow of trams through the square, you are almost sure to find fire-eaters and other street entertainers, both good and bad. By night, dazzling neon lights and crowded café terraces seating more than 1,000 people transform the square into an Amsterdam hot spot, busy until the early hours. Look for two notable buildings, both protected monuments: the distinctive redbrick Stadsschouwburg (Municipal Theatre, ▷ 93), with its wide veranda and little turrets, and the art nouveau Eden Amsterdam American hotel (▷ 112), with its striking art deco Café Americain (▷ 94).

Winter wonderland Whatever the season, Leidseplein remains one of the city's main meeting places. In winter, when most tourists have departed, it becomes quintessentially Dutch. It is the place to be for New Year's Eve celebrations—if you have a high tolerance for exploding fireworks thrown at your feet by fired-up youngsters.

Designed by Petrus Cuypers in 1885, this is the place to view the famous Night Watch

Rijksmuseum

Even in this shrunken state, the Rijksmuseum's Masterpieces collection is a glorious evocation of the Dutch Golden Age of the 17th century.

Old Masters Holland's most important museum is operating on a limited basis until at least 2013, while most of the building is being refurbished. But even when it was fully open, the Rijksmuseum could display only a fraction of its collection. Now it has been reduced to the redesigned Philips Wing, to the rear of the main building. The solution has been to display 400 of the 17th-century Old Masters paintings and other pieces from this period. Pride of place goes to Rembrandt's *The Night Watch* (1642). This vast, dramatic canvas—one of his largest and most famous compositions, portraying an Amsterdam militia company—is a showpiece of 17th-century Dutch art. In other rooms hang more works by Rembrandt and by his pupils. Jan Steen, Johannes Vermeer and Frans Hals also feature prominently. Other treasures include a collection of Delftware and two ingeniously made doll's houses—scaled-down copies of old canal houses, with sumptuous 17th-century period furnishings.

Design masterpiece Although most of the Rijksmuseum building is closed, it's still worthwhile perusing the architecture. The palatial redbrick building was designed by Petrus Josephus Hubertus Cuypers and opened in 1885. It is mostly in the style known as Dutch neo-Renaissance, but Cuypers slipped in some neo-Gothic touches.

THE BASICS

www.rijksmuseum.nl
➕ E7
✉ Jan Luijkenstraat 1
☎ 647 7000
🕐 Daily 9–6 (Fri until 8.30pm). Closed 1 Jan
🚃 Tram 2, 5
⛴ Museum Boat North/South Line stop 4
♿ Very good
✋ Expensive

HIGHLIGHTS

● *The Night Watch*, Rembrandt (1642)
● *The Jewish Bride*, Rembrandt (1665)
● *The Milk Maid*, Vermeer (1658)
● *The Love Letter*, Vermeer (1670)
● 17th-century doll's houses

Stedelijk Museum

TOP 25

© Karel Appel Foundation

THE BASICS

www.stedelijk.nl

H4

✉ Paulus Potterstraat 13
from late 2011

☎ 573 2911

🕐 Daily 10–6. Note that
the museum is closed at the
time of writing. Please check
website for reopening date

🚊 Tram 2, 3, 5, 12, 16, 24

⛴ Museum Boat North/
South Line, stop 4

♿ Moderate

💰 Expensive

❓ Lectures, films and
concerts

HIGHLIGHTS

● *The Parakeet and the
Mermaid*, Matisse (1952–53)
● *My Name as Though it
were Written on the Surface
of the Moon*, Nauman (1986)
● *Sitting Woman with Fish
Hat*, Picasso (1942)
● *Wall Painting Restaurant
Stedelijk*, Karel Appel (1956)
● *Beanery*, Kienholz (1965)
● Rietveld furniture
collection

**One of the world's leading modern art
museums. It features Henri Matisse to
Kazimir Malevich and Piet Mondrian,
and Paul Klee to Vasily Kandinsky and
Edward Keinholz.**

Controversial The Stedelijk or Municipal Museum,
Amsterdam's foremost venue for contemporary art,
was founded in 1895. In recent years, its home
base at Museumplein has been extensively
refurbished and expanded, greatly increasing the
display area, and improving access and visibility for
visitors. Its collection of more than 25,000 paintings,
sculptures, drawings, graphics and photographs
contains works by some of the great names of
modern art (Van Gogh, Cézanne, Picasso, Monet,
Chagall), but the emphasis is on progressive post-
war movements.

House of Museums In 1938 the Stedelijk
became Holland's National Museum of Modern
Art, but it achieved its worldwide avant-garde
reputation in 1945–63, when it was under the
dynamic direction of Willem Sandberg. He put
much of its existing collection in storage and
created a House of Museums in which art,
photography, dance, theatre, music and cinema
were all represented in innovative shows.

Cutting edge Museum highlights include supre-
matist paintings by Malevich; works by Mondrian,
Gerrit Rietveld and other exponents of the Dutch
De Stijl school; and a remarkable collection of
almost childlike paintings by the Cobra movement.

The park is perfect for relaxation (left); the statue of Joost van den Vondel (right)

Vondelpark

This is a popular place for sunbathers, joggers, Frisbee-throwers and book-worms. Be entertained by street players and acrobats in this welcome splash of green near the heart of the city.

Pleasure gardens With its wide-open spaces, fragrant rose garden, playgrounds, bandstand and cafés, Vondelpark is a popular place to relax. Amsterdam's largest and oldest municipal park—a 48ha (118-acre) rectangle of former marshland—was first opened in 1865. The designers, J. D. and L. P. Zocher, created an English-landscape style park with lengthy pathways, open lawns, ornamental lakes, meadows and woodland containing 120 varieties of tree. Financed by wealthy local residents, the Nieuwe Park (New Park, as it was then called) became the heart of a luxurious new residential district, overlooked by elegant town houses and villas. Two years later, a statue of Holland's best-known playwright, Joost van den Vondel (1587–1679) was erected in the park. It is the only city park in Holland that has been designated a listed monument. The park is home to the Filmmuseum (▷ 93).

Like a summer-long pop festival The heyday of Vondelpark was in the 1970s, when hippies flocked to Amsterdam, attracted by the city's tolerance for soft drugs. Vondelpark soon became their main gathering place. The bubble burst at the end of the decade and the hippies dispersed. All that remains of the spirit of that time are street musicians, flea markets and a few ageing hippies.

THE BASICS

➕ B8
✉ Stadhouderskade
🕐 Dawn–dusk
🍴 Café Vertigo (▷ 94), 't Blauwe Theehuis (▷ 92)
🚊 Tram 1, 2, 3, 5, 12
🚢 Museum Boat North/ South Line stop 3, 4
♿ Good
❓ Open-air summer festival of plays and concerts

DID YOU KNOW?

● The sumptuous art deco interior of the Dutch Filmmuseum was rescued from Amsterdam's first cinema, the Cinema Parisien. The Filmmuseum is due to move to a new building in Amsterdam-Noord (North) at the end of 2011.
● More than 1,000 new and classic films are shown here every year.

HIGHLIGHTS

- *The Potato Eaters* (1885)
- *Bedroom at Arles* (1888)
- *Vase with Sunflowers* (1888)
- *Wheatfield with Crows* (1890)

TIPS

- Arrive early (9.30am to get in by 10am) or you will find long lines.
- The best time to visit is Monday morning.

DID YOU KNOW?

- Van Gogh sold only one painting in his lifetime.
- The record price for a van Gogh painting is €56 million (1990 *Portrait of Dr. Gachet*).

It is a moving experience to trace Vincent van Gogh's tragic life and extraordinary achievement, through such a varied display of his art, his Japanese prints and his contemporary works.

World's largest van Gogh collection Of his 900 paintings and 1,200 drawings, the Van Gogh Museum has 200 and 500 respectively, together with 850 letters, Vincent's fine Japanese prints and works by friends and contemporaries, including Gauguin, Monet, Bernard and Pissarro. Van Gogh's paintings are arranged chronologically, starting with works from 1880 to 1887, a period typified by *The Potato Eaters* (1885).

Artist's palette The broad brush strokes and bold tones that characterize van Gogh's works from

People come from all over to view the most famous pictures by Vincent van Gogh, including the Sunflowers and Irises (left); the museum houses the largest collection of van Gogh's work anywhere in the world and the building has been specially designed to accommodate his art (right)

1887 to 1890 show the influence of his 1886 move to Paris and the effect of Impressionism, most striking in street and café scenes. Tired of city life, he moved in 1888 to Arles where, intoxicated by the intense sunlight and the brilliant hues of Provence, he painted many of his finest works, including *Harvest at La Crau* and the *Sunflowers* series. After snipping off a bit of his ear and offering it to a local prostitute, van Gogh voluntarily entered an asylum in St.-Rémy, where his art took an expressionistic form. His mental anguish may be seen in the way he painted gnarled trees and menacing skies, as in the desolate *Wheatfield with Crows*. At the age of 37, he shot himself.

Extra space Temporary and special exhibitions are mounted in an ellipse-shape wing designed by architect Kisho Kurokawa and opened in 1999.

THE BASICS

www.vangoghmuseum.nl
➕ D7
✉ Paulus Potterstraat 7
☎ 570 5200
🕐 Daily 10–6 (Fri until 10pm). Closed 1 Jan
🍴 Self-service restaurant
🚊 Tram 2, 3, 5, 12, 16, 24
🚢 Museum Boat North/ South Line stop 4
♿ Excellent
💲 Expensive

More to See

CONCERTGEBOUW
www.concertgebouw.nl
The orchestra and main concert hall of this elaborate neoclassical building have been renowned worldwide ever since the inaugural concert in 1888.
➕ D8 ✉ Concertgebouwplein 2–6
☎ 573 0573 🚊 Tram 3, 5, 12, 16, 24

COSTER DIAMONDS
www.costerdiamonds.com
This quality diamond workshop is one of a few in the city to give tours. The diamond business has flourished in Amsterdam since the 16th century. See the diamond cutters at work.
➕ D7 ✉ Paulus Potterstraat 2–8 ☎ 305 5555 🕐 Daily 9–5 🚊 Tram 2, 5 ♿ Few 💷 Free

HEINEKEN EXPERIENCE
www.heinekenexperience.com
An interactive introduction to the world of Heineken beer can be found in the former brewery, an uninspiring building that was producing beer until 1988. You'll see plenty about the process of brewing and old Heineken adverts. Don't miss the stables housing the Shire horses that are still used to pull the promotional drays around Amsterdam.
➕ F8 ✉ Stadhouderskade 78 ☎ 523 9222 🕐 Daily 11–7 🚊 Tram 4, 6, 7, 10, 16, 24, 25 ♿ Few (call in advance)
💷 Expensive ❓ No under 18s

MUSEUMPLEIN
This large, irregularly shaped 'square' was first laid out in 1883 and drastically rearranged in 1999. It is bordered by the Rijksmuseum (▷ 85), the Van Gogh Museum (▷ 88–89) and the modern art Stedelijk Museum (▷ 86). A rectangular pond (and winter ice-skating rink) reflects the surrounding buildings and trees at one end, and at the other is the Concertgebouw (▷ left and 93). Picnicking, Frisbee-flipping, and impromptu games of football (soccer), basketball and pétanque are popular activities.
➕ D8 ✉ Museumplein 🚊 Tram 2, 3, 5, 12, 16, 24 ⛴ Museum Boat North/South Line stop 4

The neoclassical Concertgebouw

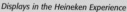

Displays in the Heineken Experience

Around the Museums and the Park

This walk enables you to visit some of the most famous museums in the city and also give you the chance to relax in the park.

DISTANCE: 3km (2 miles) **ALLOW:** 1–2 hours (plus stops)

START

RIJKSMUSEUM
✚ E7 🚊 Tram 2, 5

① Start at the park at the back of the Rijksmuseum (▷ 85) by the museum shop. Across the road is Paulus Potterstraat and Coster Diamonds (▷ 90), where you can take a tour.

② Continuing along Paulus Potterstraat you will see the Van Gogh Museum (▷ 88–89) and the Stedelijk Museum (▷ 86) on your left. Continue and turn right into Van Baerlestraat.

③ Take the first entrance into the Vondelpark (▷ 87), in front of you. Wander through the park and you will see the statue of Joost van den Vondel (▷ 87).

④ Make your way back to the original entrance. Continue round the park, passing the pavilion that houses the Filmmuseum (▷ 93).

END

RIJKSMUSEUM
✚ E7 🚊 Tram 2, 5

⑧ Continue to the junction with Hobbemastraat, where the tram rails cross, and you will find the Rijksmuseum at the end.

⑦ Turn first right onto the main street 1e Constantijn Huygensstraat taking the third left into Pieter Cornelisz Hooftstraat, one of the most exclusive shopping streets in the city; everything from Gucci to Armani is here.

⑥ This church, reminiscent of Sleeping Beauty's castle was built in 1880. About 100m (100 yards) to the left of the church is the indoor riding school, the Hollandsche Manege. Retrace your steps and head down Vondelstraat.

⑤ Leaving the park by the entrance on the right head to the Vondelkerk ahead of you.

Shopping

BLUE BLOOD
www.bluebloodbrand.com
Great designer store from
Amsterdam's Blue Blood
Jeans people, where
you'll find unique denim
items that you won't find
in London or New York.
🚇 D7 ✉ P. C. Hooftstraat
142 ☎ 676 6220 🚊 Tram
2, 3, 5, 12

DOUGLAS PARFUMERIE
www.douglas.nl
Good for big-name
scents and unpretentious
concoctions.
🚇 D7 ✉ P.C. Hooftstraat
107–109 ☎ 679 5822
🚊 Tram 2, 3, 5, 12

HERA KAARSEN
www.herakaarsen.nl
Many of the candles here
are waxen works of art
designed by the owners.
🚇 B7 ✉ Overtoom 303
☎ 616 2886 🚊 Tram 1, 6

MUSEUM SHOPS
Museum shops sell high-
quality posters of the art-
works on their walls. Look
for the best of these at the
Rijksmuseum (a small selection until the whole gallery is
reopened in 2013; at present
the shop does get very
crowded), Stedelijk Museum,
Van Gogh Museum, and
Museum Het Rembrandthuis.

IVY
www.ivy.nl
This elegant flower shop
creates floral art.
🚇 D6 ✉ Leidseplein 35
☎ 623 6561 🚊 Tram 1, 2, 5,
7, 10

OGER
www.oger.nl
One of the top menswear
boutiques and the most
conservative choice.

Precision made to meas-
ure suits can be ordered.
🚇 D7 ✉ P. C. Hooftstraat
75–81 ☎ 676 8695
🚊 Tram 2, 3, 5, 12

RETRO
www.xs4all.nl/~styles
Way-out fashion,
including a dazzling array
of 1960s and 1970s
flower-power clothing.
🚇 C6 ✉ Tweede
Constantijn Huygensstraat 57
☎ 683 4180 🚊 Tram 1, 3,
6, 12

VAN AVEZAATH BEUNE
www.vanavezaath-beune.nl
Famous for its chocolate
versions of the city's
ubiquitous anti-parking
posts, Amsterdammertjes
('little Amsterdammers'),
and other noble pralines.
🚇 C8 ✉ Johannes
Verhulststraat 98 ☎ 624
8356 🚊 Tram 2, 16

Entertainment and Nightlife

'T BLAUWE THEEHUIS
www.blauwetheehuis.nl
This 1930s pagoda-like
structure is a popular
lunch spot and place to
people-watch but it also
has a stylish upstairs bar
with a DJ starring on Friday
evenings in summer.
🚇 B8 ✉ Vondelpark 5
☎ 662 0254 🚊 Tram 1,
3, 12

BOOM CHICAGO
www.boomchicago.nl
Very popular comedy
venue with bar and
restaurant. Sketches and
improvization, all in
English every night, plus
late shows in summer.
🚇 E6 ✉ Leidseplein 12
☎ 423 0101 🚊 Tram 1, 2, 5,
6, 7, 10

BULLDOG PALACE
www.thebulldog.com
Flagship of the Bulldog
chain of bars and smok-
ing coffee shops—sells
more draft beer than
anywhere else in the city.
Downstairs is a 'smoking
coffeeshop'.
🚇 E6 ✉ Leidseplein 13–17
☎ 627 1908 🚊 Tram 1, 2, 5,
6, 7, 10

Entertainment and Nightlife

CONCERTGEBOUW

www.concertgebouw.nl
One of the world's finest concert halls, the magnificent neoclassical Concertgebouw has wonderful acoustics, making it special with musicians worldwide. Since its début in 1888, it has come under the baton of Richard Strauss, Mahler, Ravel, Schönberg and Bernard Haitink to name a few. It continues to be one of the most respected ensembles in the world, attracting renowned performers.
✚ D8 ✉ Concertgebouwplein 2–6 ☎ 671 8345 🚊 Tram 3, 5, 12, 16, 24

HOLLAND CASINO AMSTERDAM

www.hollandcasino.com
Try all the usual games, plus *Sic Bo* (a Chinese dice game) at this casino, one of Europe's largest. There is a small entrance fee and you must be over 18 and present your passport, but there is no strict dress code.
✚ D6 ✉ Max Euweplein 62 ☎ 521 1111 🚊 Tram 1, 2, 5, 7, 10

FILMMUSEUM

www.filmmuseum.nl
On the Vondelpark's northeasrtern corner you will find the imposing pavilion designed by P. J. and W. Hamer in 1881. Movies feature an international agenda and range from silent films to more recent releases.

The outdoor veranda is popular in summer for drinks.
✚ C7 ✉ Vondelpark 3 ☎ 589 1400 🚊 Tram 1, 3, 12

DE KRAKELING THEATER

www.krakeling.nl
Mime and puppet shows, for under-12s, and over-12s.
✚ D6 ✉ Nieuwe Passeerdersstraat 1 ☎ 624 5123 🕐 Phone for show times 🚊 Tram 7, 10

PARADISO

www.paradiso.nl
Amsterdam's best venue for live acts—rock, reggae and pop concerts—in a beautiful old converted church.
✚ E7 ✉ Weteringschans 6–8 ☎ 626 4521 🚊 Tram 7, 10

MELKWEG

Located in a wonderful old dairy building (hence the name Melkweg or 'Milky Way') on a canal just off Leidseplein, this off-beat multimedia entertainment complex opened in the 1960s and remains a shrine to alternative culture. Live bands play in the old warehouse most evenings, and there is also a schedule of unconventional theatre, dance, art and film events. (✉ Lijnbaansgracht 234 ☎ 5318181; www.melkweg.nl).

RENT-A-SKATE VONDELTUIN

www.skatedokter.nl
Friday night is skating night, when hundreds turn out for a mass skate from Vondelpark—when the weather is fine enough. Skates can be rented.
✚ B8 ✉ Vondelpark 7 ☎ 06 2157 5885 🚊 Tram 1, 2

STADSSCHOUWBURG

www.stadsschouwburg amsterdam.nl
Classical and modern plays form the main part of the repertoire at this stylish, 19th-century Municipal Theatre.
✚ E6 ✉ Leidseplein 26 ☎ 624 2311 🚊 Tram 1, 2, 5, 7, 10

VONDELPARK OPENLUCHTTHEATER

www.openluchttheater.nl
The open-air venue in the park offers free drama, cabaret, concerts and children's activities from June to August.
✚ B3 ✉ Vondelpark ☎ 428 3360 🚊 Tram 1, 2, 3, 5, 12

ZUIDERBAD

www.oudzuid.amsterdam.nl
This historic indoor pool (built 1912) is only a short stroll from the Rijksmuseum and is the perfect place for children to enjoy letting off steam as light relief after all that sightseeing.
✚ E7 ✉ Hobbemastraat 26 ☎ 252 1390 🚊 Tram 2, 5

Restaurants

BAGELS & BEANS (€)

www.bagelsbeans.nl
Just the place to stop for a break when visiting the Albert Cuypmarkt. Choose from all manner of bagels. Delicious muffins, great coffee and juices. Nice outdoor terrace.

➕ E8 ⊠ Ferdinand Bolstraat 70, De Pijp ☎ 672 1610
🕐 Mon–Fri 8.30–5.30, Sat–Sun 9.30–6 🚊 Tram 12, 25

BRASSERIE KEYZER (€€)

An Amsterdam institution, next door to the Concertgebouw. Fish and Dutch dishes are the specialty.

➕ D8 ⊠ Van Baerlestraat 96, Oud Zuid ☎ 675 1866
🕐 Mon–Sat 10–11, Sun 11–11 🚊 Tram 2, 3, 5, 12, 16

CAFÉ AMERICAIN (€)

www.edenamsterdam americanhotel.com
Artists, writers and bohemians have frequented this grand art deco café, ever since it opened in 1902.

➕ D6 ⊠ Eden Amsterdam American Hotel, Leidseplein 26, Leidseplein ☎ 556 3232
🕐 Daily 7am–1am 🚊 Tram 1, 2, 5, 7, 10

LE GARAGE (€€€)

www.restaurantlegarage.nl
French regional cuisine is at its best at this trendy brasserie in a converted garage near Vondelpark.

➕ D8 ⊠ Ruysdaelstraat 54–56, Oud Zuid ☎ 679 7176
🕐 Mon–Fri 12–12, Sat–Sun 6–11 🚊 Tram 3, 5, 12, 16, 24

DE OESTERBAR (€€)

www.oesterbar.nl
The seasonal delights of this elegant fish restaurant include herring in May, mussels in June and delicate Zeeland oysters throughout the summer.

➕ E6 ⊠ Leidseplein 10, Leidseplein ☎ 623 2988
🕐 Daily 12–3.30, 6–11 🚊 Tram 1, 2, 5, 7, 10

DE ORIENT (€€)

www.restaurant-orient.nl
Dark, opulent restaurant specializing in *rijsttafels*,

A BITE TO 'EET'

Try an *eetcafé* for filling, home-made fare, soup, sandwiches and omelettes. Remember that kitchens close around 9pm. Browse market stalls for local delicacies. Most bars offer *borrelhapjes* (mouthfuls with a glass)—usually olives, chunks of cheese or *borrelnoten* (nuts with a tasty coating). More substantial *borrelhapjes* are *bitterballen* (bitter balls), fried balls of vegetable paste; and *vlammetjes* (little flames), spicy mini spring rolls.

with more than 20 different varieties.

➕ D7 ⊠ Van Baerlestraat 21, Oud Zuid ☎ 673 4958
🕐 Daily 5–10 🚊 Tram 2, 3, 5, 12

RIAZ (€)

www.riaz.nl
One of Amsterdam's best Surinamese restaurants. The cooking has Creole, Javanese and Chinese influences.

➕ C6 ⊠ Bilderdijkstraat 193, Oud West ☎ 683 6453
🕐 Mon–Fri 11.30–9, Sun 2–9 🚊 Tram 3, 7, 12, 17

SAMA SEBO (€€)

www.samasebo.nl
Rush mats and batik typify this Balinese setting where you can select from the menu to create your own *rijsttafel*.

➕ D7 ⊠ P. C. Hooftstraat 27, Museumplein ☎ 662 8146
🕐 Mon–Sat 12–3, 5–10 🚊 Tram 2, 5

SMALL TALK (€€)

www.smalltalkamsterdam.nl
Eetcafé ideal for snacks between gallery visits.

➕ D8 ⊠ Van Baerlestraat 52, Oud Zuid ☎ 671 4864
🕐 Daily 8–9.30 🚊 Tram 2, 3, 5, 12

VERTIGO (€€)

www.vertigo.nl
Brown café-style, where menu-dishes occasionally reflect themes in the Filmmuseum. Lovely terrace.

➕ B8 ⊠ Vondelpark 3, Oud Zuid ☎ 612 3021 🕐 Daily 10am–1am 🚊 Tram 1, 3, 12

Just a bus or tram ride will take you into the suburbs with a plethora of windmills, the zoo and more museums. A little farther out it is easy to get to Delft or Keukenhof for a pleasant change.

NOORD

IJ - TUNNEL

JOHAN VAN
NIEUWE LEEUWARDEN
HASSELTWEG
IJSTELWEG

Het IJ

DE RUIJTERKADE

Amsterdam-Rijnkanaal

IJhaven

CENTRAAL
STATION

PRINS

PIET HEINKADE

Dijksgracht

DAMRAK

CENTRUM

HENDRIKKADE

Oosterdok

IJ-TUNNEL

KATTENBURGERSTRAAT

Wittenburgervaart

AMSTERDAM

Nieuwevaart

De Plantage

Entrepotdok

Werfmuseum
't Kromhout

AMSTEL

WATERLOO
-PLEIN

Entrepotdok

Verzetsmuseum

*Hortus
Botanicus*

*Natura
Artis
Magistra*

De Gooyer

WEESPERSTRAAT

PLANTAGE MIDDENLAAN

Artis

MAURITSKADE

Tropenmuseum

LINNAEUSSTRAAT

Singelgracht

MAURITSKADE

Oosterpark

OOST

Amstel

Albert
Cuypmarkt

WIBAUTSTRAAT

AMSTELDIJK

NOBELWEG

Sarphatipark

DE PIJP

WOUSTRAAT

RUSTRAAT

0   500 m
0   500 yds

GOOISEWEG

Tropenmuseum

Exhibits from the far-flung corners of the earth are on show at the Tropenmusem

FARTHER AFIELD ★ TOP 25

THE BASICS

www.tropenmuseum.nl
+ K7
✉ Linnaeusstraat 2
☎ 568 8200 recorded info. Junior Museum 568 8233
🕐 Daily 10–5; closed 1 Jan, 30 Apr, 5 May, 25 Dec
🍴 Ekeko restaurant
🚊 Tram 7, 9, 10, 14
♿ Very good
💰 Moderate
❓ Tropentheater

HIGHLIGHTS

- Bombay slums
- Arabian souk
- Bangladeshi village
- Indonesian farmhouse
- Indonesian *gamelan* orchestra
- Pacific carved wooden boats
- Papua New Guinean Bisj Poles
- Puppet collection

In the extraordinary Tropical Museum, once a hymn to colonialism, vibrant reconstructions of street scenes with sounds, photographs and slides evoke contemporary life in tropical regions.

Foundations In 1859 Frederik Willem van Eeden, a member of the Dutch Society for the Promotion of Industry, was asked to establish a collection of objects from the Dutch colonies 'for the instruction and amusement of the Dutch people'. The collection started with a simple bow, arrows and quiver from Borneo and a lacquer water scoop from Palembang, then expanded at a staggering rate, as did the number of visitors. In the 1920s, to house the collection, the palatial Colonial Institute was constructed and adorned with stone friezes to reflect Holland's imperial achievements. In the 1970s, the emphasis shifted away from the glories of colonialism towards an explanation of Third World problems. Beside the museum is Oosterpark, a pleasant green space.

Another world The precious collections are not displayed in glass cases, but instead are set out in lifelike settings, amid evocative sounds, photographs and slide presentations, so that you feel as if you've stepped into other continents. Explore a Bombay slum, feel the fabrics in an Arabian souk, have a rest in a Nigerian bar, contemplate in a Hindu temple or listen to the sounds of Latin America in a café. The Tropentheather, has visiting performers staging non-Western music, theatre and dance in the evenings.

More to See

1100 ROE
www.molens.nl

This old smock mill, shaped like a peasant's smock, stands 1,100 *roes* from the city's outer canal. The word *roe* means both the flat part of a sail that had to be set or reefed according to wind strength, and a unit of measurement (about 28cm/1ft) used to calculate the distance from the heart of the city.

🔁 Off map at A5 ✉ Herman Bonpad 6, Sportpark Ookmeer 🚌 Bus 19, 192, 392

1200 ROE
www.molens.nl

This early 17th-century post mill, with its impressive platform and revolving cap, was built to drain the polders.

🔁 Off map at A2 ✉ Haarlemmerweg 701 at Willem Molengraaffstraat 🚌 Bus 352, 392

ALBERT CUYPMARKT
www.albertcuypmarkt.com

Amsterdam's biggest, best-known and least expensive market, named after a Dutch landscape artist, attracts some 20,000 bargain hunters on busy days.

🔁 F8 ✉ Albert Cuypstraat 🕐 Mon–Sat 9–6 🚋 Tram 4, 16, 24, 25

AMSTELPARK

A formal rose garden and a rhododendron valley are two spectacles at this magnificent park, created in 1972 for an international horticultural exhibition. It also offers pony rides, miniature golf, a children's farm, the Rieker windmill (▷ 101) and other attractions. There is a walk for the blind, and in summer tour the park in a miniature train.

🔁 Off map at F9 🕐 Dawn–dusk 🍴 Restaurant and café 🚻 Good 🚋 Tram 4

AMSTERDAMSE BOS

Amsterdam's largest park was built on the polders outside the city in the 1930s. It is a popular weekend destination year-round. In winter, there is tobogganing and skating, in summer swimming, sailing and biking. You can also take a tram ride through the park.

🔁 Off map at A9 ✉ Amstelveen seweg 🕐 Daily dawn–dusk. Visitor area daily 12–5 🍴 Open-air pancake restaurant and café 🚌 Bus 142, 166, 170, 171, 172

Sculling down the lake in the Amsterdamse Bos

ARTIS

www.artis.nl

In addition to animals, the city zoo includes museums, an aquarium and a planetarium (hourly shows). Work continues to enhance the living conditions of some larger animals.

➕ J6 ✉ Plantage Kerklaan 38–40 ☎ 0900 278 4796 🕔 Daily 9–5 (6 in summer) 🍴 Restaurant and café 🚃 Tram 9, 10, 14 ⛴ Artis Express boat from Centraal Station (summer only) ♿ Good 💵 Very expensive

DE BLOEM

www.molens.nl

This old grain mill, built in 1768, resembles a giant pepper shaker.

➕ B2 ✉ Haarlemmerweg 465, at Nieuwpoortkade 🚌 Bus 21, 60

COBRA MUSEUM

www.cobra-museum.nl

Vividly expressionistic works by post-war CoBrA group (Copenhagen, Brussels, Amsterdam) artists Karel Appel, Asger Jorn, Pierre Alechinsky and others, are displayed at this bright white museum in Amstelveen.

➕ Off map at A9 ✉ Sandbergplein 1, Amstelveen ☎ 547 5050 🕔 Tue–Sun 11–5. Closed 1 Jan, 1 Apr, 25 Dec 🚇 Beneluxbaan 🚃 Tram 5 ♿ Excellent 💵 Moderate

ENTREPOTDOK

The old warehouses here have been converted into offices and apartments.

➕ J5 ✉ Entrepotdok 🚃 Tram 10

DE GOOYER

www.brouwerijhetij.nl

Built on a brick base in 1725, with an octagonal body and a thatched wooden frame, the windmill has been converted into a brewery and bar.

➕ K6 ✉ Funenkade 5 🕔 Fri tour 4pm 🚃 Tram 10 💵 Free

KINDERBOERDERIJ DE PIJP

www.kinderboerderijdepijp.nl

A farm especially for children, in the De Pijp district, south of the centre.

➕ F9 ✉ Lizzy Ansinghstraat 82 ☎ 664 8303 🕔 Mon–Fri 11–5, Sat–Sun 1–5 🚃 Tram 12, 25 ♿ Few 💵 Free

Line up to see the animals at Artis Zoo

De Gooyer windmill

MOLEN VAN SLOTEN

www.molenvansloten.nl

Tour round this 1847 working mill. Also has a coopery museum.

➕ Off map at A9 ✉ Akersluis 10 ☎ 669 0412 🕐 Daily 10–4.30 ♿ Good 🚋 Tram 2; bus 145, 192 💷 Moderate

DE PIJP

This lively, multicultural area was once one of Amsterdam's most attractive working-class districts outside the Grachtengordel. The bustling Albert Cuypmarkt takes place daily (▷ 99).

➕ F8 🚋 Tram 3, 4, 12, 25

DE PLANTAGE

The Plantation became one of Amsterdam's first suburbs in 1848. Before that the area was parkland.

➕ H5 🚋 Tram 9, 10, 14

DE RIEKER

The finest windmill in Amsterdam was built in 1636 to drain the Rieker polder, and is at the southern tip of Amstelpark. This was one of Rembrandt's special painting locations.

The windmill is a private home.

➕ Off map at F9 ✉ Amsteldijk, at De Borcht 🚌 Bus 62

SARPHATIPARK

A small green oasis dedicated to 19th-century Jewish doctor and city benefactor, Samuel Sarphati.

➕ F8 🕐 Daily 9–dusk 🚋 Tram 3, 25

VERZETSMUSEM

www.verzetsmuseum.org

The Resistance Museum displays rare memorabilia and a summary of the Dutch resistance during World War II.

➕ H5 ✉ Plantage Kerklaan 61a ☎ 620 2535 🕐 Tue–Fri 10–5, Sat–Sun 11–5. Closed 1 Jan, 30 Apr, 25 Dec 🚋 Tram 9, 14 ♿ Good 💷 Moderate

WERFMUSEUM 'T KROMHOUT

www.machinekamer.nl

This museum documents the development of the Eastern Islands shipbuilding industry.

➕ J5 ✉ Hoogte Kadijk 147 ☎ 627 6777 🕐 Tue 10–3 🚌 Bus 22, 43 ♿ Few 💷 Moderate

Smart conversions in the Entrepotdok

Wartime memories in the Verzetsmuseum

Excursions

THE BASICS

Distance: 55km (34 miles) southwest
Journey time: 1 hour
🚆 Train from Amsterdam Centraal Station to Delft
ℹ️ Hippolytusbuurt 4
☎ 015/215 4051; 0900 515 1555 local; www.delft.nl

Nieuwe Kerk
www.nieuwekerk-delft.nl
🕐 Apr–Oct Mon–Sat 9–6; Nov–Mar Mon–Fri 11–4, Sat 10–5 💰 Inexpensive

Oude Kerk
www.oudekerk-delft.nl
🕐 Apr–Oct Mon–Sat 9–6; Nov–Mar Mon–Fri 11–4, Sat 10–5 💰 Inexpensive

Koninklijke Porcelyne Fles
www.royaldelft.com
🕐 Guided tours Apr–Oct daily 9–5; Nov–Mar Mon–Sat 9–5. Closed 1 Jan 1, 25, 26 Dec 💰 Moderate

DELFT

This charming old town is known the world over for its blue-and-white pottery. In 1652 there were 32 thriving potteries; today there are just three.

Birthplace of the painter Jan Vermeer (1632–75) and burial place of Dutch royalty, Delft is a handsome, canal-lined town. Few of its medieval buildings survived a great fire in 1536 and a massive explosion at a powder magazine in 1654. William I of Orange (William the Silent) led his revolt against Spanish rule from the Prinsenhof in Delft. The building now houses the city museum, which includes a collection of rare antique Delftware. William is among members of the House of Oranje-Nassau who have been buried in the 14th-century Gothic Nieuwe Kerk, Holland's royal church, over the centuries. In addition, you can climb the tower of the 'New Church', which is 109m (357ft) high, for marvellous views over Delft. Vermeer is buried in the nearby 13th-century Gothic Oude Kerk, which is noted for its fine stained-glass windows. You can visit the workshop of Koninklijke Porcelyne Fles (Royal Delft), renowned makers of traditional, hand-painted Delft Blue porcelain. You get to see the pottery being made and painted, and view some fine museum pieces—and, naturally, you finish at the showroom.

THE BASICS

Distance: 26km (16 miles) southwest
Journey time: 1 hour
🚆 Train from Centraal Station to Leiden then bus direct
✉️ Lisse
☎ 0252 465555; www.keukenhof.nl
💰 Expensive

KEUKENHOF GARDENS

These gardens—whose name means 'kitchen garden'—at the heart of the Bloembollenstreek (bulb-growing region) rank among the most famous in the world.

The showcase site was bought by a consortium of bulb-growers in 1949 who saw the tourist potential. The gardens are open from mid-March to mid-May (daily 8–7.30), when more than 7 million bulbs are in bloom, laid out in brilliant swathes of red, yellow, pink and blue.

Shopping

DE BAZAAR
www.debazaar.nl
This huge indoor flea market 20km (12.5 miles) northwest of Amsterdam (reputedly Europe's largest covered market) has an Eastern Oriental Market.
⊕ Off map at A1
⊠ Industrieterrein De Pijp, Buitenland 30, Beverwijk
☎ 0251 262626 ⏰ Sat 8–6, Sun (Eastern Market only) 8–6
🚉 Beverwijk-Oost

BEETHOVENSTRAAT
www.beethovenstraat amsterdam.nl
South of the Vondelpark, this compact street has some exclusive fashion shopping and many other interesting outlets.
⊕ D9 ⊠ Beethovenstraat
🚊 Tram 5, 24

OTTEN & ZOON
Some Dutch people still clomp around in wooden *klompen* (clogs). This shop, sells fine wearable ones as well as souvenirs to take home.
⊕ F8 ⊠ Eerste Van der Helststraat 31 ☎ 662 9724
🚊 Tram 16, 24, 25

POL'S POTTEN
www.polspotten.nl
A comucopia of imaginative household fittings, both house-designed and imported, ranging from pottery to furnishings.
⊕ M4 ⊠ KNSM-laan 39
☎ 419 3541 🚊 Tram 10

SCHAAL TREINEN HUIS
www.schaaltreinenhuis.nl
Take home a windmill or canal barge kit as a souvenir. Also has model railways in stock.
⊕ C5 ⊠ Bilderdijkstraat 94
☎ 612 2670 🚊 Tram 3, 12, 13, 14

SCHIPHOL PLAZA
The large shopping mall at the airport has the longest opening hours in the city (7am–10pm).
⊕ Off map ⊠ Schiphol Airport 🚊 See transport details ▷ 116

DE WATERWINKEL
www.springwater.nl
A hundred different mineral waters to choose from, in a bright, well-lit shop. Bottles come in a range of colours.
⊕ E9 ⊠ Roelof Hartstraat 10 ☎ 675 5932 🚊 Tram 3, 5, 12, 24

Entertainment and Nightlife

AJAX AMSTERDAM
Football (soccer) is Holland's number one spectator sport and the top team is Ajax Amsterdam. Watch them play at their magnificent stadium, the Amsterdam ArenA.
⊕ Off map ⊠ ArenA Boulevard, Amsterdam Zuidoost ☎ 311 1444

AMSTERDAM BASKETBALL
www.amsterdambasketball.nl
The city's side stands tall at home games close to the Olympic Stadium.
⊕ Off map ⊠ Sporthallen Zuid, Burgerweespad 54
☎ 423 1818 🚊 Tram 16, 24

AMSTERDAM PIRATES
www.amsterdampirates.nl
The city's baseball club hits for the bleachers at a ground in the western Osdorp district.
⊕ Off map ⊠ Sportpark Ookmeer, Herman Bonpad 5
☎ 616 2151 🚌 Bus 19, 192

TICKET TIME

Tickets can be reserved directly through the Amsterdam Service Centre ☎ 551 2525. For information and tickets, contact the Amsterdams Uitburo Ticketshop (⊠ Leidseplein 26 ☎ 795 9950; www.amsterdams uitburo.nl ⏰ Office open daily 10–6, Thu until 9; phone answered 9–9 daily). Tickets can also be purchased from the VVV tourist offices.

BIMHUIS
www.bimhuis.nl
The place for followers of avant-garde and experimental jazz.
🔲 K4 ✉ Piet Heinkade 3 ☎ 788 2150 🚃 Tram 25, 26

FLEVOPARKBAD
The best outdoor swimming pool in town (mid-May to late-September).
🔲 Off map ✉ Insulindeweg 1002 ☎ 692 5030
🚃 Tram 7, 14

GOLFBAAN WATERLAND
www.golfbaanamsterdam.nl
Modern 18-hole golf course north of the city.
🔲 Off map
✉ Buikslotermeerdijk 141
☎ 636 1010 🚃 Bus 100, and all lines from 104 to 118

ICE SKATING
The canals often freeze in winter, turning the city into a big ice rink. Skates can be bought at most sports equipment stores.

JAAP EDEN IJSBANEN
www.jaapeden.nl
A large outdoor ice rink, open October to March.
🔲 M9 ✉ Radioweg 64 ☎ 0900 724 2287 🚃 Tram 9

KAMER 401
www.kamer401.nl
Relaxed hotspot in the Jordaan where you can have a drink listening to funky tunes from different DJs. Good place for pre-theatre. Open until late.
🔲 D4 ✉ Marnixstraat 401 ☎ 620 0614 🚃 Tram 3, 10

KORSAKOFF
www.korsakoffamsterdam.nl
Thrash metal and industrial sounds for the chains and piercing crowd—despite which the atmosphere is fun and friendly.
🔲 D5 ✉ Lijnbaansgracht 161 ☎ 625 7854 🕐 Tue, Fri, Sun from 10pm, Wed–Thu from 11pm, Sat from 9pm
🚃 Tram 10, 17

MALOE MELO
www.maloemelo.nl
This smoky yet convivial Jordaan bar, Amsterdam's 'home of the blues', belts out some fine rhythms from some of the best. There are occasional jam sessions.
🔲 D5 ✉ Lijnbaansgracht 163 ☎ 420 4592 🚃 Tram 3, 10

DE MIRANDABAD
Subtropical swimming pool complex with indoor and outdoor pools, beach, wave machines and a restaurant.

GAY AMSTERDAM

Clubbing is at the heart of Amsterdam's gay scene. Gay bars and clubs abound in Reguliersdwarsstraat and Halvemaansteeg. To find out exactly what's on and where it's happening, call the Gay and Lesbian Switchboard (☎ 623 6565; www.switchboard.nl) or read the bilingual (Dutch–English) magazines *Gay Krant* and *Gay&Night*.

🔲 Off map ✉ De Mirandalaan 9 ☎ 546 4444
🚃 Tram 25

MUZIEKGEBOUW AAN 'T IJ
www.muziekgebouw.nl
The innovative modern concert hall is an ocean of tinted glass on the shore of the IJ channel, east of Centraal Station. It is a major venue for contemporary classical music performances of work by John Cage, Xanakis and other pioneers, including Dutch compositions.
🔲 K4 ✉ Muziekgebouw aan 't IJ, Piet Heinkade 1 ☎ 788 2000 🚃 Tram 25, 26

RAI
www.rai.nl
This convention venue sometimes stages classical music and opera.
🔲 Off map ✉ Europaplein 22 ☎ 549 1212 🚃 Tram 4

SEASIDE
The seaside is 30 minutes away by train, with miles of clean, sandy beaches. Zandvoort is the closest resort; Bergen aan Zee and Noordwijk are also popular.
🔲 Off map 🚉 Zaandvoort aan Zee

TROPENMUSEUM
Traditional music from developing countries is played at the Tropentheater (▷ 98).
🔲 K7 ✉ Linnaeusstraat 2 ☎ 568 8500 🚃 Tram 7, 9, 10, 14

Restaurants

PRICES

Prices are approximate, based on a 3-course meal for one person.
€€€   over €50
€€   €25–€50
€   under €25

FARTHER AFIELD

AMSTERDAM (€€)

www.caférestaurantamsterdam.nl
A beautifully renovated 19th-century water-pumping station is the setting for a cool restaurant, with a menu that's a deluge of continental dishes.
⊞ D2 ⊠ Watertorenplein 6, Westerpark ☎ 682 2666 ⏰ Daily 10.30–midnight, (Fri-Sat until 1am) 🚋 Tram 10

LE CIEL BLEU (€€€)

www.cielbleu.nl
The height of stylish French cuisine on the Okura Hotel's 23rd floor.
⊞ F9 ⊠ Ferdinand Bolstraat 333, Nieuw Zuid ☎ 678 7450 ⏰ Dinner and Sun brunch 🚋 Tram 12, 25

GARE DE L'EST (€€)

www.garedelest.nl
In a former station with the policy 'you eat what cook makes'. Mediterranean style. Outdoor terrace.
⊞ L5 ⊠ Cruquususweg 9, Oost ☎ 463 0620 ⏰ Daily 6pm–10pm 🚌 Bus 43, 65

DE GOUDEN REAEL (€€)

www.goudenreael.nl
French bistro in a 17th-century dockside building with a romantic waterside terrace. Fine French regional cuisine.
⊞ E1 ⊠ Zandhoek 14, Westerdok ☎ 623 3883 ⏰ Daily 6pm–10.30pm 🚋 Tram 3; bus 48

DE KAS (€€–€€€)

www.restaurantdekas.nl
Set in a greenhouse of 1926, this trendy, out-of-the-way restaurant serves international dishes with a Mediterranean slant.
⊞ K9 ⊠ Kamerlingh Onneslaan 3, Watergraafsmeer ☎ 462 4562 ⏰ Mon–Fri 12–2, 6.30–10, Sat 6.30–10 🚋 Tram 9

PAKISTAN (€€)

www.pakistan-restaurant.com
A fine Pakistani restaurant. The menu ranges from traditional, village dishes to highly spiced specialties. It's some way out, southeast of the

SURINAMESE COOKING

Explore the narrow streets of the multiracial district around Albert Cuypstraat, and you will soon realize how easy it is to eat your way around the world in Amsterdam. The many Surinamese restaurants here serve a delicious blend of African, Chinese and Indian cuisine. Specialties include *bojo* (cassava and coconut quiche) and *pitjil* (vegetables with peanut sauce). Check out Nieuw Albina (⊠ Albert Cuypstraat 49).

Vondelpark, but worth it if this is your thing.
⊞ Off map ⊠ Scheldestraat 100, Rivierenbuurt ☎ 675 3976 ⏰ Daily 5pm–11pm 🚋 Tram 12, 25

LA RIVE (€€€)

www.restaurantlarive.nl
In Amsterdam's most expensive hotel, chef Rogér Rassin produces excellent regional French cooking.
⊞ G7 ⊠ Amstel Hotel, Prof Tulpplein 1 ☎ 520 3264 ⏰ Mon–Fri 12–2, Mon–Sat 6.30–10.30 🚋 Tram 7, 10

VISAANDESCHELDE (€€)

www.visaandeschelde.nl
This popular fish restaurant boasts an eclectic menu of fish dishes from around the world. Dine in the art deco interior or out on the patio. Just across the road from the Rai convention venue so you could combine a meal with a visit to the opera or a concert.
⊞ Off map ⊠ Scheldeplein 4, Rivierenbuurt ☎ 675 1583 ⏰ Mon–Fri 12–2.30, 5.30–11, Sat–Sun 5.30–11 🚋 Tram 4

Delft

SPIJSHUIS DE DIS (€€)

www.spijshuisdedis.com
Classy traditional Dutch restaurant where steaks are the specialty.
⊞ Off map ⊠ Beestenmarkt 36 ☎ 015 213 1782 ⏰ Thu–Tue 5–9.30 🚆 Delft

RESTAURANTS

Where to Stay

Amsterdam is probably Europe's most accessible city, and there is a range of hotels in the heart of the city, though often not enough to meet demand, so book ahead.

Staying in Amsterdam

One of the great attractions of a short break in Amsterdam is that virtually any hotel you consider will be within easy walking distance of all the main attractions. Choosing a hotel on a canal is obviously one of the nicest ideas for the location but you will pay extra. If you want peace and quiet the Museum District and the area near Vondelpark are good options.

Finding a Bargain

Two-fifths of Amsterdam's 30,000 hotel beds are classed as top-range properties, making problems for people looking for mid-range and budget accommodation. At peak times, such as during the spring tulip season and summer, empty rooms in lower-cost hotels are about as rare as black tulips. The only answer to this problem is to reserve well ahead. Special offers may be available at other times. Many hotels lower their rates in winter, when the city is far quieter than in the mad whirl of summer.

Tips for Staying

Watch out for hidden pitfalls, such as Golden Age canal houses with four floors, steep and narrow stairways and no elevator. Most of the canal-side hotels are small and only offer bed-and-breakfast. Some low-price options may not offer private bathrooms. Be wary of tranquil-looking places with a late-night café's outdoor terrace next door.

By the canal or on a street corner, hotels come in all styles and prices in Amsterdam

---

RESERVATIONS

To be sure to get the rooms you require it is essential to reserve well in advance. Hotels get fully booked months ahead, in particular those with character alongside the canals. Low season, November–March, still gets booked up as the rates drop by around a quarter. The VVV operates a hotel reservation service centre ☎ 020 551 2525—there's a €15 fee per reservation, but no fee for online reservations (www.iamsterdam.com). If you do leave it until you arrive the tourist offices make on-the-spot bookings for €4 per person.

Budget Hotels

PRICES

Expect to pay up to €125 per night for a double room in a budget hotel

ACACIA

www.hotelacacia.nl
An inexpensive, cheerful, family-run hotel with studio rentals and a pair of houseboats. 14 rooms.
➕ E3 ✉ Lindengracht 251, Jordaan ☎ 622 1460
🚊 Tram 3, 10

AMSTEL BOTEL

www.amstelbotel.com
One of Amsterdam's few floating hotels, with fine views over the old harbour. 175 rooms.
➕ H4 ✉ NDSM-Werf 3, Noord ☎ 626 4247
🚢 NDSM Ferry from Centraal Station

ARENA

www.hotelarena.nl
In a converted 19th-century orphanage, this stylish hotel has a café and restaurant. Dance nights, concerts, exhibitions. 127 rooms.
➕ J7 ✉ 's-Gravesandestraat 51, Oost ☎ 850 2400
🚊 Tram 7, 10

BELGA

www.hotelbelga.nl
A backpackers' pied-à-terre in a 17th-century building designed by Rembrandt's frame-maker, with large rooms suitable for multiple occupancy and a friendly style. 10 rooms.
➕ E4 ✉ Hartenstraat 8, Grachtengordel ☎ 624 9080
🚊 Tram 1, 2, 5, 13, 17

BICYCLE HOTEL AMSTERDAM

www.bicyclehotel.com
Small hotel that rents bikes. Maps are on offer as well as alternative routes to explore the city on two wheels. 16 rooms.
➕ F9 ✉ Van Ostadestraat 123, De Pijp ☎ 679 3452
🚊 Tram 3, 12, 25

DE FILOSOOF

www.hotelfilosoof.nl
All 38 rooms are themed after philosophers. The Vondelpark is close by as are trams to whisk you into the city. Alternatively it is a 15-minute walk.
➕ C7 ✉ Anna van den Vondelstraat 6, Oud West ☎ 683 3013
🚊 Tram 1, 6

MUSEUMZICHT

www.hotelmuseumzicht.nl
A good choice close to the Rijksmuseum, Leidseplein and Vondelpark. There are 14

CAMPING

Several campsites are in and around Amsterdam. The best equipped is out in the Amsterdamse Bos (✉ Kleine Noorddijk 1, ☎ 641 6868; www.campingamsterdamsebos.nl). Vliegenbos is close to Het IJ waterway, and the ferry to Centraal Station, in Amsterdam-Noord. (✉ Meeuwenlaan 138, ☎ 636 8855; www.vliegenbos.com).

rooms but only three have private bathrooms. No phones in the rooms either, and no elevator.
➕ D7 ✉ Jan Luykenstraat 22, Museumplein ☎ 671 2954 🚊 Tram 2, 5

PRINSENHOF

www.hotelprinsenhof.com
Comfortable and clean; one of the best budget options, on a peaceful stretch of canal. 11 rooms.
➕ G7 ✉ Prinsengracht 810, Grachtengordel ☎ 623 1772
🚊 Tram 4

STAYOKAY AMSTERDAM VONDELPARK

www.stayokay.com
A wide range of modern options, from dormitories to family rooms. 536 beds.
➕ D7 ✉ Zandpad 5, Vondelpark, Oud Zuid ☎ 589 8996 🚊 Tram 1, 2, 5, 6, 7, 10

WIJNNOBEL

www.hotelwijnnobel.com
The small townhouse rooms and basic facilities here are compensated by low cost and a location overlooking Vondelpark and close to Leidseplein. 12 rooms.
➕ D7 ✉ Vossiusstraat 9, Vondelpark ☎ 662 2298
🚊 Tram 2, 5

WINSTON

www.winston.nl
A good fun place in the Red Light District with a popular bar and club. Its rooms are funkily decorated by local artists.
➕ F4 ✉ Warmoestraat 129, Centrum ☎ 623 1380
🚊 Tram 4, 9, 14 16, 24, 25

Mid-Range Hotels

PRICES

Expect to pay between €125 and €250 per night for a double room in a mid-range hotel.

AGORA

www.hotelagora.nl
Comfortable, 18th-century canal house furnished with antiques and filled with flowers. Close to the Bloemenmarkt, this hotel couldn't be more central. 16 rooms.
➕ F6 ✉ Singel 462, Grachtengordel ☎ 627 2200
🚃 Tram 4, 9, 14, 16, 24, 25

AMBASSADE

www.ambassde-hotel.nl
Amsterdam's smartest B&B, in 10 17th-century gabled canal houses. Louis XIV-style furniture adds elegance to the 59 bedrooms.
➕ E5 ✉ Herengracht 341, Grachtengordel ☎ 555 0222
🚃 Tram 1, 2, 5

AMSTERDAM

www.hotelamsterdam.nl
Fully modernized behind its 18th-century facade, on one of the city's busiest tourist streets and with a fine restaurant, De Roode Leeuw (▷ 63). 80 rooms.
➕ F4 ✉ Damrak 93–94, Centrum ☎ 555 0666
🚃 Tram 4, 9, 14, 16, 24, 25

AMSTERDAM HOUSE

www.amsterdamhouse.com
Quietly situated small hotel beside the Amstel. Most rooms have a view of the river. 16 rooms. Apartment rentals are available.
➕ F5 ✉ 's-Gravelandseveer 3–4, Centrum ☎ 624 6607
🚃 Tram 4, 9, 14, 16, 24, 25

ATLAS

www.hotelatlas.nl
Set on the edge of the Vondelpark, this attrractive art nouveuau hotel provides a relaxing stay away from the bustle of the city. However, the popular and lively Leidseplein is only a short walk away, as is the chic designer shopping street P. C. Hooftstraat. 23 rooms.
➕ C8 ✉ Van Eeghenstraat 64, Oud West ☎ 676 6336
🚃 Tram 2, 3, 5, 12

BILDERBERG JAN LUYKEN

www.janluyken.nl
A well-run, elegant townhouse in a quiet back street near Vondelpark

ONLINE

One of the best ways to check into Amsterdam is via the Internet and there are some good websites to help. The official sites of the Amsterdam Tourism & Convention Board are a good place to start: www.iamsterdam.com and www.holland.com (▷ 115). Another good site is www.amsterdam.info/hotels (▷ 115). You will also find information on this site if you want to take a trip outside the city.

and Museumplein, not far from the Van Gogh Museum. 62 rooms.
➕ D7 ✉ Jan Luijkenstraat 58, Oud Zuid ☎ 573 0730
🚃 Tram 2, 3, 5, 12

CANAL HOUSE

www.canalhousehotel.nl
Antique furnishings and a pretty garden make this small, family-run hotel a gem. The 26 rooms are all maintained in a classic 17th-century style.
➕ E4 ✉ Keizersgracht 148, Grachtengordel ☎ 622 5182
🚃 Tram 13, 14, 17

CROWNE PLAZA AMSTERDAM CITY CENTRE

www.amsterdam-citycentre.crowneplaza.com
Centrally located, well-furnished hotel with a good range of facilities. At the top end of the mid-price range, with a roof-top terrace, swimming pool and gym. 270 rooms.
➕ F4 ✉ Nieuwezijds Voorburgwal 5, Centrum
☎ 620 0500 🚃 Tram 1, 2, 5, 13, 17

ESTHERÉA

www.estherea.nl
A well-considered blend of wood panel, canalside character that offers efficient service with modern facilities. It has been in the same family for three generations. Warm and inviting, and nice views of the canal. 71 rooms.
➕ E5 ✉ Singel 303–309, Grachtengordel ☎ 624 5146
🚃 Tram 1, 2, 5

ITC
www.itc-hotel.com
A quiet gay-orientated,
hotel, with a garden,
placed on one of the
city's most beautiful
canals. 20 rooms.
➕ G7 ✉ Prinsengracht 1051,
Grachtengordel ☎ 623 0230
🚋 Tram 4

LLOYD HOTEL
www.lloydhotel.com
In a refurbished monu-
ment of Amsterdam
School architecture from
1921, this innovative
hotel has 117 rooms with
free wi-fi and 24-hour
room service.
➕ L4 ✉ Oostelijke
Handelskade 34, Oostelijke
Eilanden ☎ 561 3636
🚋 Tram 10, 26

NH DOELEN
www.nh-hotels.com
Amsterdam's oldest hotel,
where Rembrandt painted
the *Night Watch*; 85 small
well-equipped rooms.
➕ F5 ✉ Nieuwe
Doelenstraat 26, Centrum
☎ 554 0600 🚋 Tram 4, 9,
14, 16, 24, 25

NH SCHILLER
www.nh-hotels.com
Built in 1912, this hotel in
the Rembrandtplein with
its bars, restaurants and
outdoor café terraces,
epitomizes the art deco
period. The renovation of
the rooms is sympathetic,
retaining many of the
original elements. 92
rooms.
➕ F6 ✉ Rembrandtplein 26,
Rembrandtplein ☎ 554 0700
🚋 Tram 4, 9, 14

NOVA
www.novahotel.nl
A clean, simple, central
hotel with 61 rooms and
a friendly young staff in
a peaceful location behind
the Royal Palace.
➕ F4 ✉ Nieuwezijds
Voorburgwal 276, Centrum
☎ 623 0066 🚋 Tram 1, 2, 5

OWL
www.owl-hotel.nl
In a quiet street near
Vondelpark, this family-
owned hotel has 34
bright rooms and a
pretty garden.
➕ D7 ✉ Roemer
Visscherstraat 1, Oud Zuid
☎ 618 9484 🚋 Tram 2, 3,
5, 12

PRINS HENDRIK
www.hotel-prinshendrik.nl
Opposite Centraal Station,
the Prins Hendrik offers
a warm welcome and
newly renovated rooms
all with bathrooms. Some
rooms have great views
of the Amsterdam skyline.
There are also an intimate

ALTERNATIVES
If you want to rent an
apartment in Amsterdam,
contact Amsterdam House
(☎ 626 2577; www.
amsterdamhouse.com); you
can take your pick of luxury
apartments in converted
canal houses. Bed and
Breakfast Holland
(☎ 0497 330300;
www.bedandbreakfast.nl)
will set you up with a room
in a private house.

bar and a restaurant. 30
rooms.
➕ G4 ✉ Prins Hendrikkade
52–57, Centrum ☎ 623 7969
🚋 All trams to Centraal
Station

SEVEN BRIDGES
www.sevenbridgeshotel.nl
Small and exquisite; the
owners treat their guests
like friends. With its position on the city's prettiest
canal, this is everyone's
special bed-and-breakfast
with many guests return-
ing. 11 rooms.
➕ F7 ✉ Reguliersgracht 31,
Grachtengordel ☎ 623 1329
🚋 Tram 4

SINT NICOLAAS
www.centrehotels.nl
In the unlikely setting of
a cosily converted rope
factory, this hotel has 27
individually styled rooms,
some with exposed wood
beams, and in-room
saunas at the high end
of the price range.
➕ F3 ✉ Spuistraat 1a,
Centrum ☎ 626 1384
🚋 Tram 1, 2, 5, 13, 17

VONDEL
www.hotelvondel.com
A boutique hotel dating
from 1903 inside five
houses in a quiet street
near the Vondelpark. It is
very convenient for
Leidseplein and the
museums. The 67 rooms
are stylish.
➕ D7 ✉ Vondelstraat
28–30, Oud West ☎ 515
0455 🚋 Tram 1, 6

Luxury Hotels

PRICES

Expect to pay over €250 per night for a double room in a luxury hotel.

BANKS MANSION

www.banksmansion.nl
The 51 rooms in this ultra-stylish hotel don't come cheap but everything is included, even the minibar, bar snacks and drinks in the lounge. Total indulgence.
⊞ F6 ⊠ Herengracht 519-525 ☎ 420 0055 🚊 Tram 16, 24, 25

BILDERBERG GARDEN

www.gardenhotel.nl
In a pleasant suburb, a short tram ride from the heart of the city. 124 rooms. Check it out for special deals off-season.
⊞ C9 ⊠ Dijsselhofplantsoen 7, Oud Zuid ☎ 570 5600 🚊 Tram 5, 16, 24

THE DYLAN

www.dylanamsterdam.com
This stunning 17th-century conversion was designed by Anouska Hempel. The 41 rooms should be seen to be believed. It occupies a secluded but central spot.
⊞ E5 ⊠ Keizersgracht 384, Grachtengordel ☎ 530 2010 🚊 Tram 1, 2, 5

EDEN AMSTERDAM AMERICAN HOTEL

www.edenamsterdam
americanhotel.com
A resplendent art nouveau Amsterdam classic sited on the Leidseplein. 175 rooms.
⊞ D6 ⊠ Leidsekade 97, Grachtengordel ☎ 556 3000 🚊 Tram 1, 2, 5, 6, 7, 10

HOTEL DE L'EUROPE

www.leurope.nl
Prestigious, combining turn-of-the-20th-century architecture with the most modern amenities, in a waterfront setting. 100 rooms.
⊞ F5 ⊠ Nieuwe Doelenstraat 2–8, Centrum ☎ 531 1777 🚊 Tram 4, 9, 14, 16, 24, 25

INTERCONTINENTAL AMSTEL

www.amsterdam.
intercontinental.com
Holland's most luxurious and expensive hotel. 79 rooms.
⊞ G7 ⊠ Prof Tulpplein 1, Amstel ☎ 622 6060 🚇 Weesperplein 🚊 Tram 6, 7, 10

BIJOU HOTELS

Staying in a hotel with character is high on the agenda for many people visiting Amsterdam, especially one on a canal. Hotels in the city are often in old buildings, former warehouses or merchants' homes. Some of these have been converted to a very high standard and ooze class. So for a room with a view of the water you are spoiled for choice. Elegant canals to overlook include Keizergracht, Singel and Prisengracht.

NH GRAND HOTEL KRASNAPOLSKY

www.nh-hotels.com
Built in the 1880s, the 'Kras' has Belle Époque grace in its public spaces and modern facilities in its rooms. 468 rooms.
⊞ F4 ⊠ Dam 9, Centrum ☎ 554 9111 🚊 Tram 4, 9, 14, 16, 24, 25

PULITZER

www.starwoodhotels.com
Twenty-four 17th-century houses have been converted into this luxurious canalside hotel. Split level and wooden beams retain an authentic Dutch ambience. 230 rooms.
⊞ E5 ⊠ Prinsengracht 315–331, Grachtengordel ☎ 523 5235 🚊 Tram 13, 14, 17

SEVEN ONE SEVEN

www.717hotel.nl
Luxurious bed-and-breakfast that feels like you are staying in the private home of a wealthy family. Eight rooms and suites are themed after painters, authors and composers.
⊞ E6 ⊠ Prinsengracht 717, Grachtengordel ☎ 427 0717 🚊 Tram 1, 2, 5

SOFITEL AMSTERDAM THE GRAND

www.sofitel.com
From 16th-century royal inn to City Hall; now a luxury hotel with a strong sense of history. 178 rooms.
⊞ F5 ⊠ Oudezijds Voorburgwal 197, Centrum ☎ 555 3111 🚇 Nieuwmarkt

Readily accessible by plane, boat and train, Amsterdam has the added bonus of having excellent public transportation and is easy to walk around. Take care walking at night, especially in the Red Light District.

Planning Ahead

When to Go

Most tourists visit Amsterdam between April and September; late March to late May is the time to see tulips in bloom. June brings the Holland Festival of art, dance, opera and plays. Although winter can be cold and damp, December is crowded with Christmas shoppers and those staying for the festive season.

TIME

Amsterdam is 1 hour ahead of London, 6 hours ahead of New York and 9 hours ahead of Los Angeles.

AVERAGE DAILY MAXIMUM TEMPERATURES

JAN	FEB	MAR	APR	MAY	JUN	JUL	AUG	SEP	OCT	NOV	DEC
41°F	43°F	48°F	55°F	63°F	68°F	72°F	72°F	68°F	57°F	46°F	41°F
5°C	6°C	9°C	13°C	17°C	20°C	22°C	22°C	20°C	14°C	8°C	5°C

Spring (March to May) is at its most delightful in May—with the least rainfall and the crowds not so intense as the summer months.

Summer (June to August) is the sunniest time of year but good weather is not guaranteed.

Autumn (September to November) gets wetter, although September is a popular time to visit. The weather is often chilly and drizzly as winter approaches.

Winter (December to February) can be cold, and temperatures can drop so low that the canals freeze. Strong winds can increase the chill factor, and fog can blot out the sunlight for days.

WHAT'S ON

February *Chinese New Year*: In Chinatown (around Zeedijk).

March *Stille Omgang* (2nd Sat night): Silent procession.

April *National Museum Weekend*: Museums lower entrance fees.
Koninginnedag (30 Apr): The official Queens' birthday and day of celebrations.

May *Remembrance Day* (4 May): Pays tribute to World War II victims.
Liberation Day (5 May): Marking the end of the German Occupation in 1945.

National Windmill Day (2nd Sat).
National Cycling Day (2nd Sun).

June *Holland Festival*: International arts festival.

July *Over Het IJ Festival* (early Jul): 10 days of contemporary theatre, music and dance, at the NDSM-Werf, Amsterdam-Noord.

August *Amsterdam Pride* (early Aug): one of Europe's biggest gay festivals with the spectacular Canal Parade.
Grachtenfestival (mid-Aug): this annual canal festival

culminates with the *Prinsengracht-concert*, classical music recitals on barges outside the Hotel Pulitzer.

September *National Monument Day* (2nd Sat): Buildings open to the public, with free admission..
Jordaan Festival (2nd week): Music, street parties.

November *Sinterklaas* (Santa Claus) Parade (mid-Nov).

December *Oudejaarsavond* (31 Dec): Street parties, fireworks.

Useful Websites

www.channels.nl
Use this website to take a virtual walk around the city. Pick any street and the site will display photographs and links to hotels, museums, shops or restaurants on that street. The forum is full of useful hotel and restaurant reviews written by visitors to Amsterdam.

www.amsterdam.info
www.hotels.nl
Accommodation sites: The first site represents a cross-section of hotels in the city, from budget to deluxe, including apartments and houseboats. The second covers the whole of the Netherlands, and is useful if you want to travel farther afield or find hotels in nearby towns when all the hotels in Amsterdam are full. Both sites have up-to-date details of tariffs, special offers and room availability, with pictures of typical rooms on offer and maps showing the precise location.

www.iamsterdam.com
www.holland.com
Official tourist board sites: The first covers Amsterdam and the second the whole of the Netherlands. They are good for information about exhibitions, events and festivals. Both have online hotel booking.

www.dinnersite.nl
Say what kind of food you like and you'll get a comprehensive list of Amsterdam restaurants to suit. More than 10,000 restaurants are featured on this site, covering all the Netherlands, and you can specify criteria such as 'child friendly' or 'wheelchair accessible'. You can also use the site to make reservations online.

www.bma.amsterdam.nl
For everything you could ever want to know about the architecture in Amsterdam, visit this excellent and informative site belonging to Amsterdam Heritage.

PRIME TRAVEL SITES

www.fodors.com
A complete travel-planning site. You can research prices and weather; book air tickets, cars and rooms; pose questions (and get answers) to fellow visitors; and find links to other sites.

www.eurostar.com
For details of international rail services.

www.ns.nl
Journey planner for getting around Holland by train.

www.hollandsepot. dordt.nl
Fascinating information (mostly in Dutch) on traditional Dutch food, with recipes.

INTERNET CAFÉS

City Games Internet Café
www.citygamesinternet.tk
✉ Sint-Antoniesbreestraat 3
🕐 Daily 10–10

The Internet Café
www.internetcafé.nl
✉ Martelaarsgracht 11
🕐 Sun–Thu 9am–1am,
Fri–Sat 9am–3pm

The Mad Processor
www.madprocessor.nl
✉ Kinkerstraat 11–13
🕐 Tue–Sun 2pm–midnight

Getting There

VISAS AND TRAVEL INSURANCE

For the latest passport and visa information, look up the British embassy website at www.britishembassy.gov.uk or the United States embassy at www.usembassy.state.gov. EU citizens can obtain health care with the production of the EHIC card. However, insurance to cover illness and theft is strongly advised.

DRIVING

If you do bring a car you can follow the excellent electronic signage for parking as you come into the city but be prepared as there is often a shortage. Driving is not an ideal way of getting about the city because of the scarcity and high cost of public parking, the one-way narrow and congested streets and the large number of cyclists. Cars are generally discouraged and any penalities incurred will be high. During the annual Queen's Day celebrations around 30 April, many city roads are closed to traffic. Never drive under the influence of alcohol.

AIRPORTS

There are direct international flights into Schiphol Airport from around the world, as well as good rail connections with most European cities and regular sailings from the UK to major ferry ports, all of which have good rail connections to Amsterdam.

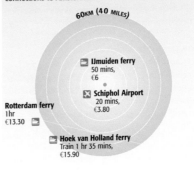

60KM (40 MILES)

IJmuiden ferry
50 mins,
€6

Schiphol Airport
20 mins,
€3.80

Rotterdam ferry
1hr
€13.30

Hoek van Holland ferry
Train 1 hr 35 mins,
€15.90

FROM SCHIPHOL

Schiphol (☎ 0900/0141; www.schiphol.nl), Amsterdam's only international airport, is 13km (8 miles) southwest of the heart of the city. Many international airlines operate scheduled and charter flights here. Trains leave the airport for Amsterdam Centraal Station every 10 minutes from 6am until midnight, then hourly through the night. The ride takes 20 minutes and costs €3.80. Connexxion Hotel Shuttle buses run from the airport to more than 100 hotels and you can request a hotel if it is not on the list. The cost is €14.50 one-way, €22.50 return; 6am–9pm (☎ 038 339 4741; www.schipholhotelshuttle. nl). You should never have to wait more than 30 minutes for a bus and they can be every 10 minutes. It leaves outside Arrivals 2. Taxis are available but fares run as high as €50. It is faster to go by train to Centraal Station and take a taxi from there.

ARRIVING BY RAIL

Centraal Station has direct connections from major cities in western Europe, including high-speed links from Paris, Brussels and Cologne.

From Britain, there are connections at Brussels with trains operated by Eurostar, with bargain through fares to Amsterdam. Train information: (☎ 0900/9296; www.ns.nl).

CENTRAAL STATION

Whether you come from the airport or the ferry port, or on an international train, you will end up at this station (▷ 51). A few tips can help you avoid problems on arrival:

● Once off the platforms the main concourse is crowded with visitors and loiterers.

● The station is a magnet for pickpockets and hustlers who target tourists.

● Tourist information is upstairs on Platform 2 and outside the station on Stationsplein.

● Heading out of the main entrance you will be confronted with a confusion of taxis, trams, buses and bicycles.

● The main taxi rank is to the right of the main entrance as are tram stands 1, 2, 5, 13 and 17.

● To the left are tram stands 4, 9, 16, 24, 25 and 26, and the entrance to the Metro.

● Just beyond is the city's main tourist office (VVV) in a white-painted wooden building.

● To the left is the GVB Tickets & Info public transportation office, where you buy travel passes and reserve tickets for canal cruises (🕙 Mon–Fri 7am–9pm, Sat, Sun 10am–6pm).

● Water transportation options are the Canal Bus, Museum Boat, Water Taxi, canal-boat tours, and, at the rear of the station, passenger ferries and two-wheel transportation to three different points on the north bank of Het IJ.

ARRIVING BY SEA

The major ferry ports—IJmuiden (23km/14 miles), Rotterdam Europoort (70km/43 miles) and Hoek van Holland (Hook of Holland, 68km/42 miles)—have good rail connections with Amsterdam. Regular sailings from the UK are offered by Stena Line (☎ 08447 707070; www.stenaline.co.uk), DFDS Seaways (☎ 0871 522 9955; www.dfds.co.uk) and P&O Ferries (☎ 08716 645645; www.poferries.com).

CUSTOMS

Allowances (17 years up)
Goods Bought Outside the EU (Duty-Free Limits):
Alcohol: 1 litre of spirits over 22% volume, OR 2 litres of fortified wine, sparkling wine or other liqueurs, PLUS 2 litres of still table wine
Tobacco: 200 cigarettes, OR 100 cigarillos, OR 50 cigars, OR 250g of tobacco
Perfume: 50ml
Toilet water: 250ml

Goods Bought Inside the EU for Your Own Use (Guidance Levels):
Alcohol: 10 litres of spirits AND 20 litres of fortified wine, sparkling wine or other liqueurs, AND 90 litres of wine, AND 110 litres of beer
Tobacco: 800 cigarettes, AND 400 cigarillos, AND 200 cigars, AND 1kg of tobacco

Not allowed:
Drugs, firearms, ammunition, offensive weapons, obscene material, unlicensed animals including birds and insects

CAR RENTAL

You will find the usual leading international rental companies both at Schiphol Airport and in the city.

Getting Around

CANAL TRAVEL

You can buy an all-day ticket for the Canal Bus although the route and schedules are not too easy to follow. The Museumboot operates from Centraal Station and stops at seven tourist points around the city. Water taxis have to be reserved in advance and are expensive. See panel opposite for more details.

TRAMS AND BUSES

Sixteen different tram lines have frequent services from 6am on weekdays (slightly later on weekends) until 12.15am. In addition, there are dozens of city (GVB) and regional (Arriva and Connexxion) bus services. A service of 12 night bus lines operates in the city from about 12.30am to to about 6.30am. Day tickets are valid during the night following the day on which they were issued. It is best to buy your ticket in advance but for a single journey you can pay the conductor. Take care when getting off; many stops are in the middle of the road. For maps and timetables, and much more city public transportation information, go to www.gvb.nl.

METRO

There are four Metro lines, three terminating at Centraal Station, used mainly by commuters from the suburbs. The most useful city stations,in addition to Centraal Station, are Nieuwmarkt and Waterlooplein.

TAXIS

Taxis are plentiful, though not used as often as in most other cities because of the nature of Amsterdam's streets and canals. Traffic easily becomes congested, and it can be quicker to walk, cycle or take public transportation. Taxi fares are quite high. You can call a taxi by ringing the main city taxi company, TCA (☎ 0900 677 7777 (extra-charge priority line) or 777 7777). There is a taxi rank outside the Centraal Station, and a few others around the city, including at Leidseplein and Rembrandtplein, and you can also hail a cab on the streets.

TICKETS

● Like all other *openbaar vervoer* (public transportation) companies in the Netherlands, GVB Amsterdam is introducing the new OV-chipkaart (chipcard) as a way of paying for using the city's Metro, tram and bus services (and NS/Dutch Railways trains).

- The OV-chipkaart is being phased in. When deployment of the electronic stored-value card is complete—possibly by the end of 2010—the old system of fare zones and *strippenkaart* (strip card) tickets will be discontinued. At the time of writing, the chipcard is the only way to pay for the Metro, and it is no longer possible to buy a *strippenkaart* on trams and buses.
- Three main types of OV-chipkaart are available: a reloadable 'personal' card (€7.50 for the card plus up to €30 worth of travel) that can be used only by the person whose picture is on the card; a reloadable 'anonymous' card (€7.50 for the card plus up to €30 worth of travel), which can be used by anyone; and, for limited use, 'throwaway' cards (€2.50 and €4.80), which, unlike the other two cards, can only be used with the company of purchase.
- Electronic readers at Metro and train stations, and on trams and buses, deduct the fare, which is calculated per kilometre.
- GVB Amsterdam day and multi-day cards—which function like chipcards—may be simpler and more-cost-effective for visitors making frequent use of the city's public transportation. These cards cost: 24 hours (€7.50), 48 hours (€11.50), 72 hours (€15), 96 hours (€18), 120 hours (€23), 144 hours (€26), 168 hours (€29).
- Buy OV-chipkaart and other cards from GVB Tickets & Info (see below) and Metro stations.
- Don't travel without a valid ticket: You will be fined €35 on the spot.
- For further information and maps, contact GVB Tickets & Info ✉ Stationsplein ☎ 0900/9292 (Dutch only); www.gvb.nl.

GETTING AROUND BY BICYCLE

- The best way to see Amsterdam is by bicycle. There are penty of cycle lanes, distances are short and there are no hills.
- To rent a bike costs from €10 a day, €40 a week: Damstraat Rent-a-Bike ✉ Damstraat 20–22 ☎ 625 5029, www.bikes.nl ⏰ Daily 9–6; Bike City ✉ Bloemgracht 68–70 ☎ 626 3721, www.bikecity.nl ⏰ Daily 9–6.

ORGANIZED SIGHTSEEING

Canal boats are not a part of the public transporation system and although quite expensive are a wonderful way to see the city. The busiest canal-boat docks are those at Centraal Station and on nearby Damrak. Other docks around the city are Rokin, Leidseplein and Stadhouderskade (at Ferdinand Bolstraat).

Holland International
☎ 625 3035; www.canal.nl. Cruises every 20 min in summer; every 30 min in winter.

Canal Bus
☎ 623 9886; www.canal.nl Water-bus service around the city. Hop on-and-off day pass is a good option.

Lovers
☎ 530 1090; www.lovers.nl Tours daily 9–6, every 30 min.

Museum Line
☎ 530 1090; www.lovers.nl 10 stops linking the major museums. Service every 30–45 min.

OTHER OPTIONS

Yellow Bike Tours
✉ Nieuwezijds Kolk 29
☎ 620 6940;
www.yellowbike.nl

Walking tours
Mee in Mokum
✉ Keizersgracht 346
☎ 625 1390;
www.meeinmokum.nl
Tours Mon–Fri 1–4

Essential Facts

MONEY

The euro is the official currency of the Netherlands. Bank notes are in denominations of 5, 10, 20, 50, 100, 200 and 500 euros and coins in denominations of 1, 2, 5, 10, 20 and 50 cents and 1 and 2 euros.

10 euros

50 euros

200 euros

500 euros

MONEY MATTERS

Banks may offer a better exchange rate than hotels or independent bureaux de change. GWK Travelex (Grenswisselkantoor) offer 24-hour money-changing services at Schiphol Airport and extended hours at Centraal Station and in many locations around the city.

ELECTRICITY
● 230 volts; round two-pin sockets.

MEDICINES
● For nonprescription drugs, and so on, go to a *drogist*. For prescription medicines, go to an *apotheek*, most open Mon–Fri 8.30–5.30.
● Details of pharmacies open outside normal hours are in the daily newspaper *Het Parool* and all pharmacy windows.
● Outside normal working hours, Amsterdam Doctors Service (☎ 088 0030600; www.shda.nl) can refer you to a GP (*huisarts*) or dentist (*tandarts*).
● Hospital (*ziekenhuis*) outpatient clinics are open 24 hours. The most central is Onze-Lieve-Vrouwe Gasthuis ✚ J7 ✉ Oosterpark 9 ☎ 599 9111; www.olvg.nl 🚊 Trams 3, 10, 17.

NATIONAL HOLIDAYS
● 1 January; Good Friday, Easter Sunday and Monday; 30 April; Ascension Day; Pentecost Sunday and Monday; 25 and 26 December.
● 4 and 5 May—Remembrance Day (*Herdenkingsdag*) and Liberation Day (*Bevrijdingsdag*)—are World War II Commemoration Days.

NEWSPAPERS AND MAGAZINES
● The main Dutch newspapers are *De Telegraaf* (right wing), *De Volkskrant* (left wing) and *NRC Handelsblad.*
● The main Amsterdam newspaper is *Het Parool.*
● Listings magazines: *Amsterdam Day by Day, Amsterdam Weekly* and *Uitkrant* (monthly).
● Foreign newspapers are widely available.

OPENING HOURS
● Banks: Mon–Fri 9 until 4 or 5. Some stay open Thu until 7.
● Shops: Tue–Sat 9 or 10 until 6, Mon 1 to 6. Some open Thu until 9 and Sun noon until 5. Some close early Sat, at 4 or 5.
● State-run museums and galleries: most open

Tue–Sat 10 to 5, Sun and national holidays
1 to 5. Many close on Mon.

PLACES OF WORSHIP
● Roman Catholic: Sint-Nicolaaskerk:
✉ Prins Hendrikkade 73 ☎ 330 7812;
www.nicolaas-parochie.nl
● English Reformed Church: ✉ Begijnhof 48
☎ 624 9665; www.ercadam.nl
● Jewish: Portugese Synagoge: ✉ Mr
Visserplein 3 ☎ 624 5351; www.esnoga.com
● Muslim: Moskee Djame Masdjied Taibah:
✉ Kraaiennest 125 ☎ 698 2526; www.taibah.nl

POST OFFICES
● Most post offices open weekdays 8.30 or 9
until 5.
● Main Post Office: ✚ E4 ✉ TNT Post Singel
250 ☎ 0900 767 8526 🕔 Mon–Fri 7.30–12,
12.30–6.30, Sat 7.30–9.30.
● Postal Information: ☎ 058 233 3333
● Purchase stamps (*postzegels*) at post offices,
tobacconists and souvenir shops.
● Post boxes are orange.
● For overseas mail use the *overige
bestemmingen* slot.

TELEPHONES
● Most public telephones take phonecards
available from telephone hubs, post offices,
rail stations and newsagents.
● National directory enquiries: ☎ 0900 8008
● International directory enquiries: ☎ 0900
8418
● Numbers starting 0900 are premium rate;
0800 are free; 06 are mobile phone numbers.
● Local/international operator: ☎ 0800 0410
● To phone abroad, dial 00 then the country
code (UK 44, US and Canada 1, Australia 61,
New Zealand 64, Ireland 353, South Africa 27),
then the number.
● Most hotels have International Direct
Dialling, but it is expensive.
● The code for Amsterdam is 020. To phone
from outside Holland drop the first 0.

STUDENTS

For discounts at some
museums, galleries, venues,
restaurants and hotels,
students under 26 can obtain
an International Young
Person's Pass (CJP–Cultureel
Jongeren Pass), cost €15
from: AUB ✉ Leidseplein 26
☎ 0900/0191

LOST PROPERTY

● For insurance purposes,
report lost or stolen property
to the police as soon as
possible.
● Main lost property offices:
Centraal Station
✚ G3 ✉ Stationsplein 15
☎ 557 8544 🕔 Daily 8–8
● Police Lost Property
✚ E6 ✉ Korte
Leidsedwarsstraat 52
☎ 251 0222 🕔 Mon–Fri
9–4
● For property lost on public
transport, GVB ✚ Off map,
west of A2 ✉ Arlandaweg
100 ☎ 0900 8011
🕔 Mon–Fri 9–4

SENSIBLE PRECAUTIONS

● Pickpockets are common in busy shopping streets and markets, and in the Red Light District. Take sensible precautions and remain on your guard at all times.

● At night, avoid poorly lighted areas and keep to busy streets. Amsterdam is not dangerous, but muggings do occur.

● There are enhanced risks to women travelling alone. Public transportation is generally busy even late at night. A rented bicycle (or a taxi) can obviate the need for using infrequent night buses or walking alone in quiet or deserted areas.

TOILETS

● There are few public toilets. Your best bet is to use the facilities in museums, department stores and the bigger hotels. There is often a small charge (€0.30–€0.50).

TOURIST OFFICES (VVV)

● The ATCB's three Vereniging voor Vreemdelingenverkeer (VVV) tourist information offices and the Holland Tourism International desk at Schiphol Airport all have multilingual staff (all offices ☎ 0900 400 4040 inside the Netherlands; 31-20 551 2525 outside the Netherlands; www.iamsterdam.com). They make hotel, excursion, concert and theatre reservations for a small fee:
Centraal Station 🚇 G3 ✉ Centraal Station, Platform 2;
Stationsplein 🚇 G3 ✉ Stationsplein 10;
Leidseplein 🚇 D6 ✉ Facing Stadhouderskade 1 (white kiosk);
Holland Tourism International (HTI)
🚇 Off map ✉ Schiphol Airport.

EMERGENCY PHONE NUMBERS

Police, ambulance, fire	☎ 112
Amsterdam Doctors Service	☎ 088 0030600
Automobile Emergency (ANWB)	☎ 088 269 2888
Lost credit cards	American Express ☎ 504 8666, Diners Club ☎ 0800 555 1212 Master/Eurocard ☎ 0800 022 5821, Visa ☎ 0800 022 3110
Victim Support	☎ 0900 0101
Crisis Helpline	☎ 675 7575

EMBASSIES AND CONSULATES

American Consulate	✉ Museumplein 19 ☎ 575 5309
Australian Embassy	✉ Carnegielean 4a, The Hague ☎ 070 310 8200
British Consulate	✉ Koningslaan 44 ☎ 676 4343
Canadian Embassy	✉ Sophialaan 7, The Hague ☎ 070 311 1600
Irish Embassy	✉ Dr. Kuyperstraat 9, The Hague ☎ 070 363 0993
New Zealand Embassy	✉ Eisenhowerlaan 77n, The Hague ☎ 070 346 9324
South African Embassy	✉ Wassenaarseweg 40, The Hague ☎ 070 392 4501

Language

BASICS

ja	yes
nee	no
alstublieft	please
bedankt	thank you
hallo	hello
goedemorgen	good morning
goedemiddag	good afternoon
goedenavond	good evening
welterusten	good night
dag	good-bye

USEFUL WORDS

goed/slecht	good/bad
groot/klein	big/small
warm/koud	hot/cold
nieuw/oud	new/old
open/gesloten	open/closed
ingang/uitgang	entrance/exit
heren/damen	men's/women's
wc	lavatory
vrij/bezet	free/occupied
ver/dichtbij	far/near
links/rechts	left/right
rechtdoor	straight ahead

NUMBERS

een	1
twee	2
drie	3
vier	4
vijf	5
zes	6
zeven	7
acht	8
negen	9
tien	10
elf	11
twaalf	12
dertien	13
veertien	14
vijftien	15
zestien	16
zeventien	17
achttien	18
negentien	19
twintig	20
dertig	30
veertig	40
vijftig	50
honderd	100
duizend	1,000

USEFUL PHRASES

Spreekt u engels?	Do you speak English?
Zijn er nog kamers vrij?	Do you have a vacant room?
met bad/douche	with bath/shower
Ik versta u niet	I don't understand
Waar is/zijn?	Where is/are ..?
Hoe ver is het naar?	How far is it to ..?
Hoeveel kost dit? ...	How much does this cost?
Hoe laat gaat u open?	What time do you open?
Hoe laat gaat u dicht?	What time do you close?
Kunt u mij helpen?	Can you help me?

DAYS AND TIMES

Zondag	Sunday
Maandag	Monday
Dinsdag	Tuesday
Woensdag	Wednesday
Donderdag	Thursday
Vrijdag	Friday
Zaterdag	Saturday
vandaag	today
gisteren	yesterday
morgen	tomorrow

Timeline

BEFORE 1400

Herring fishermen settle on the Amstel in the 13th century and a dam is built across the river. In 1300 the settlement is given city status and in 1345 becomes an important pilgrimage place and a major trading post, although remaining very small.

HERRING CITY

If there had been no herring, Amsterdam might never have come into existence. In the Middle Ages, the Dutch discovered how to cure these fish, and they became a staple food. Herring fishermen built a dam across the Amstel river and a small fishing village developed, Amstelledamme. Its site is now the Dam, Amsterdam's main square.

1425 First horseshoe canal, the Singel, is dug.

1517 Protestant Reformation in Germany. In subsequent decades Lutheran and Calvinist ideas take root in the city.

1519 Amsterdam becomes part of the Spanish empire and nominally Catholic.

1567–68 Start of the Eighty Years' War against Spanish rule.

1578 Amsterdam capitulates to William of Orange. Calvinists take power.

17th century Dutch Golden Age. Amsterdam becomes the most important port in the world.

1602 United East India Company founded. It collapses in 1799.

1613 Work starts on the Gratchtengordel (Canal Ring).

1642 Rembrandt paints his classic work *The Night Watch*.

1648 End of war with Spain.

1652–54 First of a series of wars with Britain for maritime supremacy.

1806 Napoleon takes over the republic.

1813 Prince William returns from exile. Crowned William I in 1814.

1876 North Sea Canal opens, bringing new prosperity.

1914–18 World War I. The Netherlands is neutral.

1928 Amsterdam hosts the Olympics.

1940–45 German Occupation in World War II. Anne Frank goes into hiding.

1960s–70s Hippies flock to the city from around Europe.

1964–67 Antiestablishment riots are rife.

1980 Queen Beatrix crowned. The city is named Holland's capital.

1989 City government falls because of weak anti-vehicle laws. New laws aim to eventually free the city of traffic.

1990 Van Gogh centenary exhibition attracts 890,000 visitors.

1998–99 Redevelopment of Museumplein.

2011 The modern-art Stedelijk Museum is due to reopen at its Museumplein home, after an extensive renovation and expansion project.

A POPULAR MONARCH

Beatrix, Queen of the Netherlands, came to the throne when her mother Queen Juliana, abdicated on 30 April 1980. Beatrix, born in 1938, was inaugurated at the Nieuwe Kerk. Her great popularity is reflected on her official birthday (*Koninginnedag*, 30 April)—an exuberantly celebrated national holiday.

From far left: Napoleon Bonaparte; ornate ceramic panel with portrait of artist Frans Hals; waiting outside the Anne Frank' House; statue of Rembrandt; Neptune at the Amsterdam Maritime Museum

Index

INDEX

Amsterdam's
25 BEST

WRITTEN BY Teresa Fisher
ADDITIONAL WRITING Hilary Weston and Jackie Staddon
UPDATED BY George McDonald
DESIGN WORK Jacqueline Bailey
COVER DESIGN Tigist Getachew
INDEXER Marie Lorimer
IMAGE RETOUCHING AND REPRO Sarah Montgomery and James Tims
REVIEWING EDITOR Linda Schmidt
PROJECT EDITOR Bookwork Creative Associates Ltd
SERIES EDITOR Marie-Claire Jefferies

ISBN 978-1-4000-0537-6

EIGHTH EDITION

IMPORTANT TIP
Time inevitably brings changes, so always confirm prices, travel facts, and other perishable information when it matters. Although Fodor's cannot accept responsibility for errors, you can use this guide in the confidence that we have taken every care to ensure its accuracy.

SPECIAL SALES
This book is available for special discounts for bulk purchases for sales promotions or premiums. Special editions, including personalized covers, excerpts of existing books, and corporate imprints, can be created in large quantities for special needs. For more information, write to Special Markets/Premium Sales, 1745 Broadway, MD 6–2, New York, NY 10019 or email specialmarkets@randomhouse.com.

Color separation by AA Digital Department
Printed and bound by Leo Paper Products, China
10 9 8 7 6 5 4 3 2 1

A04202
Maps in this title produced from mapping © MAIRDUMONT / Falk Verlag 2011
Transport map © Communicarta Ltd, UK

The Automobile Association wishes to thank the following photographers, companies and picture libraries for their assistance in the preparation of this book.

Abbreviations for the picture credits are as follows – (t) top; (b) bottom; (l) left; (r) right; (c) centre; (AA) AA World Travel Library

1 AA/M Jourdan; 2 AA/M Jourdan; 3 AA/Jourdan; 4t AA/M Jourdan; 4c AA/A Kouprianoff; 5t AA/M Jourdan; 5c AA/K Paterson; 6t AA/M Jourdan; 6cl AA/A Kouprianoff; 6cr AA/A Kouprianoff; 6bl AA/A Kouprianoff; 6br AA/A Kouprianoff; 7t AA/M Jourdan; 7cl AA/A Kouprianoff; 7c AA/K Paterson; 7cr AA/A Kouprianoff; 7bl AA/M Jourdan; 7bc AA/M Jourdan; 7br AA/M Jourdan; 8 AA/M Jourdan; 9 AA/M Jourdan; 10t AA/M Jourdan; 10ct AA/M Jourdan; 10c AA/K Paterson; 10cb AA/K Paterson; 10b AA/M Jourdan; 11t AA/M Jourdan; 11ct AA/M Jourdan; 11c AA/M Jourdan; 11cb AA/M Jourdan; 11b AA/M Jourdan; 12 AA/M Jourdan; 13t AA/M Jourdan; 13ct AA/W Voysey; 13c AA/A Kouprianoff; 13cb Digital Vision; 13b AA/K Paterson; 14t AA/M Jourdan; 14ct AA/M Jourdan; 14c AA/K Paterson; 14cb AA/K Paterson; 14b AA/M Jourdan; 15 AA/M Jourdan; 16t AA/M Jourdan; 16ct AA/K Paterson; 16cb AA/K Paterson; 16b AA/K Paterson; 17t AA/M Jourdan; 17ct AA/K Paterson; 17c AA/A Kouprianoff; 17cb AA/K Paterson; 17b AA/M Jourdan; 18t AA/M Jourdan; 18ct AA/M Jourdan; 18c AA/K Paterson; 18cb AA/M Jourdan; 18b AA/K Paterson; 19t AA/A Kouprianoff; 19ct AA/A Kouprianoff; 19c AA/M Jourdan; 19cb AA/K Paterson; 19b AA/M Jourdan; 20/21 AA/K Paterson; 24 AA/K Paterson; 24/25 Anne Frank House (photographer Allard Bovenberg); 25 Anne Frank House (photographers Allard Bovenberg); 26l AA/K Paterson; 26r AA/K Paterson; 27l AA/K Paterson; 27c AA/M Jourdan; 27r AA/K Paterson; 28 AA/A Kouprianoff; 29t AA/M Jourdan; 29bl AA/A Kouprianoff; 29br Circus Elleboog (photographer Jean van Lingen); 30t AA/M Jourdan; 30b AA/M Jourdan; 31 AA/K Paterson; 32 AA/K Paterson; 33 AA/M Jourdan; 34 AA/K Paterson; 35 AA/A Kouprianoff; 36 AA/K Paterson; 37 AA/M Jourdan; 40l AA/M Jourdan; 40/41 AA/K Paterson; 40r AA/K Paterson; 41t AA/K Paterson; 41bl AA/K Paterson; 41br AA/K Paterson; 42l AA/A Kouprianoff; 42r AA/A Kouprianoff; 43l AA/M Jourdan; 43r AA/K Paterson; 44l AA/A Kouprianoff; 44c AA/K Paterson; 44r AA/K Paterson; 45l AA/K Paterson; 45r AA/K Paterson; 46l AA/K Paterson; 46r AA/K Paterson; 47l AA/K Paterson; 47r AA/K Paterson; 48l AA/M Jourdan; 48c AA/K Paterson; 48r AA/K Paterson; 49 AA/M Jourdan; 50l AA/K Paterson; 50r AA/K Paterson; 51t AA/M Jourdan; 51b AA/A Kouprianoff; 52t AA/M Jourdan; 52bl AA/A Kouprianoff; 52br AA/K Paterson; 53t AA/M Jourdan; 53bl AA/M Jourdan; 53br AA/K Paterson; 54 AA/K Paterson; 55 AA/M Jourdan; 56 AA/M Jourdan; 57 AA/M Jourdan; 58 Brand X Pictures; 59 Photodisc; 60t Brand X Pictures; 60c AA/C Sawyer; 61 AA/A Kouprianoff; 62 Photodisc; 63 AA/C Sawyer; 64 AA/A Kouprianoff; 65 AA/K Paterson; 68l Jewish Historical Museum (on loan from NIHS, Amsterdam); 68r Jewish Historical Museum (Photo: Liselore Kamping); 69l AA/K Paterson; 69r AA/K Paterson; 70l AA/K Paterson; 70c AA/M Jourdan; 70r AA/K Paterson; 71l AA/M Jourdan; 71r AA/K Paterson; 72 AA/K Paterson; 72/73 AA/K Paterson; 74l AA/W Voysey; 74r AA/A Kouprianoff; 75t AA/M Jourdan; 75bl AA/K Paterson; 75br AA/K Paterson; 76t AA/M Jourdan; 76bl AA/M Jourdan; 76br AA/K Paterson; 77t AA/M Jourdan; 77bl AA/K Paterson; 77br AA/K Paterson; 78 AA/A Kouprianoff; 79 AA/A Kouprianoff; 80 AA/K Paterson; 81 AA/K Paterson; 84l AA/A Kouprianoff; 84r AA/K Paterson; 85l AA/K Paterson; 85r AA/K Paterson; 86/87 AA/M Jourdan; 87 AA/M Jourdan; 88 AA/A Kouprianoff; 88/89 AA/A Kouprianoff; 90t AA/M Jourdan; 90bl AA/K Paterson; 90br AA/K Paterson; 91 AA/K Paterson; 92t AA/K Paterson; 92c Digital Vision; 93 Digital Vision; 94 Imagestate; 95 AA/M Jourdan; 98l AA/M Jourdan; 98r AA/A Kouprianoff; 99t AA/M Jourdan; 99b AA/A Kouprianoff; 100t AA/M Jourdan; 100bl AA/M Jourdan; 100br AA/M Jourdan; 101t AA/M Jourdan; 101bl Verzetsmuseum; 101br AA/A Kouprianoff; 102t AA/M Jourdan; 102b AA/K Paterson; 103 AA/M Jourdan; 104t Photodisc; 104c AA/T Souter; 105 Brand X Pictures; 106 AA/C Sawyer; 107 AA/A Kouprianoff; 108t AA/C Sawyer; 108ct AA/K Paterson; 108c AA/C Sawyer; 108cb AA/S McBride; 108b AA/A Kouprianoff; 109 AA/C Sawyer; 110 AA/C Sawyer; 111 AA/C Sawyer; 112 AA/C Sawyer; 113 AA/K Paterson; 114 AA/K Paterson; 115 AA/K Paterson; 116 AA/K Paterson; 117 AA/K Paterson; 118 AA/K Paterson; 119 AA/K Paterson; 120t AA/K Paterson; 120b www.euro.ecb/int; 121t AA/K Paterson; 121b AA/W Voysey; 122 AA/K Paterson; 123 AA/K Paterson; 124t AA/K Paterson; 124bl AA; 124bc AA/K Paterson; 124/125 AA/K Paterson; 125t AA/K Paterson; 125bc AA/A Kouprianoff; 125br AA/K Paterson

Every effort has been made to trace the copyright holders, and we apologise in advance for any unintentional omissions or errors. We would be pleased to apply any corrections in any following edition of this publication.